GIRLS GONE WILD

In the twisted little movie inside Elisa's head, she and Sarah were starring as Thelma and Louise. In the fantasy, torqued and tweaked by the marijuana and other drugs, Larry had become, in Elisa's eyes, just another bad man out to do her harm. Sarah eagerly encouraged that perception, nurturing the smallest grudge against Larry into full-fledged hatred while at the same time extending a hand of friendship to Elisa in order to help her through her trials and tribulations, real and imagined.

Some of Sarah's co-workers say that she and Elisa were as close as "husband and wife" after Sarah had been working at the firm a little more than two months. Those who saw them said Sarah definitely "wore the pants" in the relationship, controlling and influencing Elisa far more effectively than Larry could.

That was the source of the problem. Sarah ran Elisa, and Larry was cut out. His inability to deal with the issue effectively gave the keys to the kingdom not only to Elisa, but also eventually to Sarah. And they both proved to have the hearts of pirates.

MARKED
FOR DEATH

BRIAN J. KAREM

AVON BOOKS
An Imprint of HarperCollinsPublishers

AVON BOOKS
An Imprint of HarperCollins*Publishers*
10 East 53rd Street
New York, New York 10022-5299

Copyright © 2005 by Brian J. Karem
ISBN: 0-06-052471-5
www.avonbooks.com

First Avon Books paperback printing: June 2005

Avon Trademark Reg. U.S. Pat. Off. and in Other Countries, Marca Registrada, Hecho en U.S.A.
HarperCollins® is a registered trademark of HarperCollins Publishers Inc.

Printed in the U.S.A.

10 9 8 7 6 5 4 3 2 1

For, Pam, Zachary, Brennan, Wyatt, and the family.
With a special thank-you to Dr. Michael Slack,
who helped save Wyatt's life.

Contents

Author's Note

For many years Laren Sims adopted a variety of personalities. The most common was Elizabeth Barasch, a name she stole from a fellow inmate in prison. She shortened the name to Elisa and married twice under that name. There were dozens of other aliases, but in telling this story it would become very confusing to use them all interchangeably. I have instead opted to use the name "Laren" to describe her in her early life before she went on the road and on the run. I have used "Elisa" to cover the time when she was on the run and living in Las Vegas and later in the Sacramento area. Finally, I returned to calling her "Laren" when she was captured and back in jail in Florida.

I hope this cuts down on the confusion for the reader.

MARKED
FOR DEATH

Introduction

Regarding many of the events that occurred in this book, there remains no effective way of determining the veracity of certain factual claims. Laren Sims was a parasitic chameleon who lied with an ease that many who investigated her had never seen before.

She was a real-life Zelig with dark overtones; a con artist who eluded the law successfully for a decade and managed to persuade two intelligent and respectable men into marrying her even after she got caught red-handed stealing money from *both* of them.

She was described as breathtakingly beautiful, while others didn't think she was much to look at. However, everyone who knew her said she was conniving, clever, intelligent, and able to con anyone. In the end, her greatest con job may have been on herself.

As the final events of her life unfolded, her third husband, Larry McNabney, was dead. She had confessed to his murder, and then took her own life in a jail cell not fifteen minutes from where she lived as a girl. The only other person to witness most of the events prior to and including Larry's poisoning on September 10, 2001, was Sarah Dutra, Laren's secretary.

A younger, apparently more lethal version of Laren Sims, according to her prosecutors, and as stunning, Sarah is currently serving more than eleven years behind bars for her participation in Larry's death.

Any claims she makes of a factual nature are even more suspect than Laren's. So again we must conclude that all claims of fact are not as they seem. There are, however, certain undisputed facts. Larry McNabney is dead. Laren Sims is dead. Sarah Dutra is in jail. The only survivor of those turbulent times is Laren's daughter, Haylei Jordan, who made a fresh start in Florida.

With that said, there are some logical conclusions we can draw about what happened. Laren Sims's latest host, who had been her husband, divorced her and wanted her out of his life. She needed someplace to land, and Larry McNabney was a man with some local celebrity and, more important for Laren, money. Perhaps she went looking specifically for Larry. It would be within her character. Then again, there is no way of knowing if their meeting was anything more than a random twist of fate.

But the facts clearly show that once Laren found Larry, she sank her teeth into him and didn't let him go until he was dead.

She used a variety of tools to control people, and those tools enabled her to take advantage of him. Nothing Laren Sims did from the time she fled Florida had the ring of honesty to it. Everything she said and did had an ulterior motive to it. She was a talker, and she had sizable female attributes. She also didn't hesitate to use everyone around her, even her daughter, in a bid to get what she wanted. Her narcissism knew no bounds.

Eventually, using and shedding aliases with the ease and frequency of a master magician, Laren would work her way back to Florida from California while the police were engaged in a nationwide hunt for her. Part of it was fear, no doubt. But she didn't run for the border, and she never tried to flee the country when it was well within her ability to do so.

Controlling events to the last, she headed home, perhaps for the sake of her daughter. And maybe she wanted to run home to Mom and Dad too, that in the end her family was all Laren ever wanted, recognizing the value of her upbringing when it was too late.

Prosecutors and police, among others, believed that Laren had an ulterior motive in mind even then. It remains a possibility, but in any case, in the end Laren was stripped to the bone. She was spent. Stripped of all pretense, of all luxury, she was reduced to living in homeless shelters and upon the kindness of strangers. And by then she had nothing more in mind than to get her child to safety. Or at least I choose to believe so. Again, with so many conflicting stories spun about Laren Sims, it's hard know what the truth was. Maybe she went home to get a rest, dump her daughter off, and then flee again.

Even the honorable Bernard J. Garber, of the Superior Court of the State of California in San Joaquin

County, thought it was problematic, at best, to discover the truth behind any of Laren's actions. He viewed a videotaped confession after she was arrested in Florida, but didn't allow it to be introduced as evidence in the state's case against Sarah Dutra. His decision was based on the fact that it was hearsay evidence, and because of Laren's lack of credibility. "You talk about a life being a lie," he said, "that was Elisa McNabney." Judge Garber was referring to one of Laren's many aliases.

He viewed the tape and found that some facts checked out, but when it came to the actual events of the murder, "where [Laren] directly implicates the defendant [Sarah Dutra] in the actual killing of the victim, I have wondered and wondered was that true. And my answer is: I don't know."

His most damning judgment was equally harsh: "They say that a dying declaration is admissible because most people aren't willing to meet their maker with a lie upon their lips. I don't think that would apply to Elisa McNabney."

So if I fall victim to believing one of Laren's lies, I will not be the first, and probably not the last. But I'd like to think that with all she did, she had one decent act in her. I want to believe she ultimately gave up and turned herself in while trying to get her daughter to safety.

I hope for her daughter's sake Haylei believes that too.

1

You Bitches Will Never Get Away with This

September 10, 2001

Larry McNabney knew he was being murdered for close to the last twenty-four hours of his life, and as those hideous and horrendous final scenes played out, he also knew the torture of being unable to do anything about it.

Compounding his agony, both physical and mental, was the fact that he knew that not only was he dying, but that his own wife was killing him. Elisa, a beautiful woman almost eighteen years his junior, had slowly and proficiently poisoned him.

She had help, and Larry knew who that was too— his own secretary, Sarah, a woman he had never liked. The two women coldly laughed at his futile struggles to save himself and made fun of him as they watched his life slowly but surely ebb from his lethargic body.

They had all traveled to Industry City, California,

outside of Los Angeles, a place that accurately con-
jures up in the imagination a rustic yet dusty blue-
collar town. Larry had gone there with his wife, his
secretary, and his beloved quarter horses for a horse
show that week. He loved the time he spent on the road
with horses Skye Blue Summer, Ima Town Celebrity,
and the award-winning two-year-old Justa Lotta Page.
His growing infatuation with his quarter horses not
only made him beloved on the circuit and a minor
celebrity, but he was becoming an owner of champions
of the breed. Larry and his horse trainer and good
friend Greg Whalen were so proud of what they'd accomplished they'd recently discussed trying to win the
world title. It was the latest turn in the life of a person
who was described by his former partner as a "magic
man."

Larry McNabney had overcome adversity all his
life. He'd battled his own personal demons, which
came with the death of his father and older brother.
He'd defeated bouts of depression and alcoholism to
become a well-known, well-heeled lawyer who wined
and dined with the rich and the powerful and became
one of them. Yet, even as a member of the elite, he did
not become an elitist. He counted people from all
walks of life as friends, among them judges, politicians, police, bartenders, clients, and other lawyers.

But in the end the trappings of the good life and the
accolades he earned could offer him no help when he
needed it most.

He sat in a heap in the backseat of his own red
pickup truck and glanced over to see his wife, Elisa,
talking to his secretary Sarah as she drove away from

Industry City to points unknown. It was the ultimate
humiliation. He was an inanimate object sitting there.
He tried to speak but could only slur the words. He
tried to move, but could only flail about uncontrollably.
The horse tranquilizer his wife and secretary had been
feeding him from a Visine bottle, one drop at a time,
was sapping him of his strength, energy, coordination,
and ability to fight back. The only thing left was his
will to live. As he looked around, he let out a gasp and
a moan. Perhaps he saw the new shovels in the back of
the pickup, a chilling indication of what the two
women had in mind for him.

"Can you imagine the torture Larry felt at that
point?" his ex-wife JoDee Bebout later said. "He was a
vivacious man, and he was reduced to moaning for
help while the people who supposedly cared for him
the most laughed about killing him."

Larry's wife and secretary had begun hatching their
plan before the trip to Industry City. Later there would
be speculation that they had already begun to slowly
poison him, weeks, even months, before they finally
gave him the fatal dose. In any case, once Larry and
Elisa were there for the horse show, the final curtain
came down. Sarah drove down from the Sacramento
law office on September 10 and joined Elisa. Together,
while Larry dozed in his modest hotel room—in a typical middle-priced room with beige and tan window
and wall dressings—they stood over his sleeping body
and in a nonchalant, almost cavalier fashion talked
about killing him.

"We said that nobody would miss him because
everybody hated him, and we said if we kill him, no-

body's gonna miss him . . ." his wife would tell later police.

Sarah, the secretary who had convinced Elisa that Larry was evil incarnate, talked about smothering him with his pillow while he slept. But the women thought he might wake up and overpower them. They also rejected using a gun. It was too messy—and not very ladylike. Elisa would tell police that she didn't like the brutality of a gun, so they settled on slipping him the horse tranquilizer. It seemed a peaceful, easy way to kill someone.

"We went down to my trainer's truck, and I got the medicine bag out, and I got the tranquilizer out of it, and I got a syringe, and I went back over to my truck and said I don't know how we're gonna do it to him," she said.

But the crafty, inventive secretary had a keen idea. "Sarah said put it in the Visine bottle," Elisa explained.

So, as Larry slept, they squirted three drops of highly potent horse tranquilizer into his mouth. Elisa said she "freaked out" as the liquid came out slower than she expected. "I was squeezing and I thought it's not coming out, it's not coming out, and I saw a drop go and a drop go . . ." Eventually the strain was too much for her, and she handed the bottle to Sarah who, Elisa says, calmly administered a few drops more.

Then they decided to watch their handiwork. For a while they were almost convinced Larry was dead, but he wasn't. Although Sarah and Elisa tell different stories, they both agreed that they initially failed to kill Larry; they only doped him so strongly that he resembled a zombie. Elisa said he begged to die, and then, she claims, he got violent and began to threaten her. In her confession, she seemed to use this as justification for killing him. Though it seems illogical to think that someone could go from being a zombie to being violent, Elisa also neglected to mention that if indeed he became violent, it was probably because he was scared and desperately clinging to life. To Elisa and Sarah, Larry's violence was just another indication of "what an asshole he was."

Much later, when she was facing the possibility of life behind bars, Sarah told a different story, pinning the responsibility for everything on Elisa, saying she was in fear of her own life from Elisa McNabney. Neither story fits the facts, nor explains some key events that happened that week.

Those people who knew Larry and saw him at the horse show said he hadn't been himself the entire time he was there. Adding fuel to the speculation that the two women had been slowly poisoning him for some time, some of his friends and acquaintances say that in fact Larry hadn't been himself for weeks before the horse show. All independent witnesses agree that on Sunday, September 9, 2001, Larry was drinking heavily at dinner. He had successfully battled alcoholism for years, so his friends were distressed to see him so obviously and staggeringly drunk. They concluded that something must've been wrong.

Indeed, he may have already been poisoned by the time he got to Industry City and checked into his hotel, slowly poisoned, as the prosecutors suspected, for days or weeks prior to the day he died. The poison may have been slipped into a drink or administered by drops in his mouth as he slept in his hotel room, as his wife later said, but whatever the truth might have been, Larry seemed more and more lethargic, and those who saw him on September 10 said he appeared disheveled and disoriented.

When he awoke in his hotel room after being poisoned, Elisa said that he began to moan and gasp, saying, "I'm dying. I'm dying."

But apparently he wasn't dying fast enough for Elisa or Sarah, because they administered more horse tranquilizer even after he woke up. They gave him drop after drop on into the night. The next morning, September 11, 2001, as they watched the World Trade Center buildings topple in New York City, they decided to get Larry out of the hotel.

But in his state of lethargy, Larry was difficult to move. He was a tall man, trim from years of physical activity, but solidly built, and the two women, slim and not particularly athletic, needed help. So Sarah, under Elisa's guidance, rented a wheelchair and brought it up to the hotel room.

In a bold and audacious move, the women plopped Larry—who was in no condition to argue—into the wheelchair and rolled him downstairs to the pickup truck. Their trek took them out of the hotel room, down the hall, into the elevators, and out the front door. If anyone asked, the women were perfectly willing to say that Larry was drunk and had fallen off the wagon again. No one stopped them, and they managed to get him into the truck.

Then they took off.

They must have been quite a sight to see. The driver,

Sarah, in her early twenties, was a young, vivacious blonde who had more than a passing resemblance to the actress Jennifer Aniston. Sarah's best friend and confidante, Elisa was in her mid-thirties, a gorgeous brunette, at the time, who it seemed could change her hair color and hair length at will. Some said she changed her looks like others changed their underwear. A tall, leggy woman with large breasts, she dressed professionally and always looked well put together. "She had a sassy flair with a lot of class," one of her husband's law clients said.

In the back of the truck, groggy, frumpy, and dressed in anything but the manner of a well-known, well-groomed lawyer, was Larry.

They drove for hours, making their way toward Yosemite National Park. On the drive north they continued to administer the horse tranquilizer to Larry until Elisa saw some "white stuff" on the edge of his mouth. They stopped for gas at one point and switched drivers. Elisa remembered Sarah trying to hold Larry in the backseat and then finally hanging him on the truck's clothes hook as he desperately fought to get into the front seat and gain control of the pickup.

Elisa said Larry was struggling because he hated Sarah, but prosecutors would say it was something much more personal, that in all likelihood he was fighting for his life, and losing to two very conniving, beautiful, and ultimately lethal women.

When they got to Yosemite, a park Sarah had visited many times as a child, she pulled off the main road and found a wooded area far from the beaten path. No one else was around, and the quiet forest with its tall trees

and leafy, soft soil provided the perfect cover for what
the two women had in mind. Elisa later told police that
Sarah got out of the truck, grabbed one of the shovels,
and had started to dig a hole near the pickup truck,
when she stopped her. Larry, hanging on the clothes
hook in the truck, was still alive and still struggling.

"I said, we can't put him in there, he's alive, we can't
do that," Elisa explained.

Sarah, she said, was perfectly willing to bury Larry
alive, but after a shrill and angry diatribe, Elisa dis-
suaded her. Perhaps Elisa's arguments swayed Sarah,
or perhaps Sarah feared the screaming would bring un-
wanted attention to what they were doing. In any event,
Sarah quit digging the hole, got back inside the truck
and continued to drive. To Elisa it was obvious that
they couldn't bury Larry alive. They had to wait. They
had to kill him.

Larry now came around again and struggled, fu-
tilely, to free himself. He had enough energy to begin
shouting at the two women.

"You bitches will never get away with this!" he exclaimed.

The declaration shook both women to the core. Elisa
told police that Larry once again tried to attack Sarah.
Amazingly, Elisa also said the attack was "unpro-
voked." Later he began mumbling incoherently, over
and over again, "Why Blanch? Why Blanch? What are
you doing to me, Blanch?" Blanch was a nickname
Larry had given Elisa in memory of a Bette Davis
character in a movie.

Despite his condition, doped to the gills, it took
them a while to subdue him. Leaving Yosemite, they

decided to take Larry to his Woodbridge, California, home outside of Lodi. He and Elisa lived near a golf course, and there was a wooded area not far from the home. They could bury Larry there, if he died. But what if he didn't die? The repercussions were staggering. Elisa said she thought about calling poison control, but changed her mind. "I wanted him to die," she coldly told police later.

But Larry, weighing around 200 pounds and more than six feet tall, still didn't die.

Elisa said the ten-hour drive home taxed her beyond belief, and while Larry drew labored breaths in the back of the pickup, Sarah took the time to assuage Elisa's concerns. "Just calm down. Just calm down," she told Elisa as they watched Larry struggling for his life in the back of the truck.

They eventually pulled the pickup into the garage of Elisa and Larry's three-bedroom home adjacent to the golf course. There was a large, wide refrigerator in the garage; Larry's favorite set of expensive golf clubs; rakes and lawn equipment; and ski gear. The women dragged him past the material reminders of his comfortable existence and took him up to his room. His wife would later describe him as looking as if he had a stroke. He seemed to be suffering from Bell's palsy, a condition where half the face sags uncontrollably while the other side remains unaffected. The results can be hideous to look at in its worst stages. Half the face nearly melts away while the other half remains stoically unaware of the event.

About that time, Elisa claims Larry "pissed himself," so she changed him into some rudimentary bedclothes and attempted to help him—even bathing him. "I was always having to take care of him," she told police of the man she helped murder. Part of her concern for her husband extended to wiping his mouth, since the white foam was still appearing at the corners. Then again, she also said her actions weren't necessarily to help him; she just didn't like the way it looked.

For her part, Sarah appeared so unconcerned with Larry that she left for a time to drive home and pick up her prized dog, Ralphie, a Maltese. She would cite her profound love for her pet dog, but seemed to have no compassion for her boss and best friend's husband, who was slowly, painfully, dying a little bit each minute.

She didn't care.

Elisa didn't care either. They left Larry facedown on the bare floor in his bedroom.

They both woke up the next morning and switched on the television set to see more about the mass murder that had occurred the preceding morning when the World Trade Center's twin towers toppled down. Fascinated by the news and the live pictures of the smoking buildings—not to mention the people hanging out of the windows in futile attempts to obtain help—the two women couldn't pull themselves away from the television set. There, on the small screen, was a scene as horrific as Pearl Harbor. They both remember being immensely moved to sadness thinking about all the people who died as the towers crashed to the ground on live television and countless news reporters across the country replayed the event every few minutes just a day later. It was a moving and profoundly sad moment in the history of the country. Almost as an afterthought, they checked in to see Larry.

On the morning of September 12 he was dead in his own bedroom.

For Elisa and Sarah, the only concern now was what to do with the body.

2

Small Town

On the outside she was calm, but on the inside she was a maze of interconnected neurons firing indiscriminately.

—A friend describing Laren Sims

Central Florida in the late 1960s was at a crossroads. Post-WWII society, more interconnected than any in the history of man, was in the process of changing the South. Florida, arguably, saw the most radical changes as people from all over the country sought refuge in the sun. The snowbirds, the drifters, the rich, the poor, the uneducated and the educated—anyone and everyone made their way to the Sunshine State for the weather and the beaches.

By the end of the decade, as Neil Armstrong was making his historic walk on the moon, and the Beatles were busy breaking up, and young Tom Petty was growing up in gator country, just a few years away from releasing "American Girl," a young American girl by the name of Laren Sims was witnessing the changes of the South firsthand. The change was inescapable to most, and seemingly unobtainable to her. She wasn't the specific girl Tom Petty would sing about, but he obviously knew her type. She was an American girl raised on promises, and everywhere she looked, as Tom Petty wrote, she couldn't help but thinking there was more to life somewhere else.

Miami was a boomtown, while places like Fort Lauderdale and Daytona—with its car race—were attracting the young college and high school springbreak crowds. NASA had taken over places like Cocoa Beach and Cape Canaveral, where the Kennedy Space Center was the hub of a huge influx of engineers, pilots, and other service personnel and their families.

For a young girl in a backwater town like Brooksville, Florida, the romance was alluring and painful. In the 1960s, Brooksville was still a small town, little more than a county square surrounded by a dusty country road. Today, Brooksville, and all of Hernando County, is a bustling bedroom community just north of Tampa. While it still retains its charm and small-town grace, as the county seat, Brooksville has also experienced the predictable infusion of strip malls, fast-food palaces, Wal-Marts, and widened roads with greater volumes of traffic. The rustic atmosphere of the 1960s is almost hard to imagine. Back then, there was no action for a girl like Laren Sims, who desperately craved it. Brooksville was nowhere, and Laren wanted to be somewhere—anywhere—else.

For those unfamiliar with the difference between

Brooksville now and then, one merely has to see a picture of the old sheriff's department to get a glimpse into the changes. In a nutshell, it tells the story of Hernando County during the last forty years, with the population explosion that has occurred since then. In fact, to even see the photograph, you'd have to park off a main thoroughfare—a divided highway—and pull into a large parking lot complete with landscaping that highlights one of the picturesque cypresses in the area. Then you'd have to walk through the double doors of the current sheriff's department, into a large entrance foyer with high ceilings, nice tile, and large windows. At the information booth you'd see the old sheriff's office in a picture hanging to the right.

It was a white *house*.

A nice-sized one, but not exceedingly so.

There was a stone planter on the front porch, as well as a rocking chair and a Pepsi machine. The county had enough money back then to air-condition the jail, but it was a window unit, not central air-conditioning.

The jail took up a portion of the house, and the two sheriff's deputies parked on a gravel patch in back. The sheriff's wife—as many in the sheriff's department will tell you—fed all of the inmates herself. Times were rare then when the county had more than four or five prisoners, and even rarer still were the times when the sheriff's wife didn't cook for the inmates, not only because she was a good cook, but also because she lived in the house, as did the sheriff. The entire sheriff's staff back then couldn't fill out a softball team. Today, there are hundreds of people working in the sheriff's office.

To say life in Hernando County was rustic is an understatement. In fact, until Larry McNabney was found dead at the hands of his fugitive felonious Floridian wife, the largest news story to hit Brooksville was nearly 140 years old. In 1864, during the Civil War, Union troops had raided the area with the second U.S. Colored Infantry to try and break up supply and communications lines. Workers at the city's library proudly point out that it was "a very famous local battle."

But other than that, the area had been notoriously quiet. Until the last decade, the sheriff's department had no need for anything larger than the big white house in the old photographs. Mayberry, that mythical small town inhabited by Barney Fife and Andy Taylor, was not unlike Brooksville, Florida, in the 1960s. There were only five thousand people in the whole county in 1965. "In the sixties there were more cows than people in Hernando County," says Joe Paez, the sheriff's department spokesman. Compare that to the year 2000, when there were more than 140,000 people in the county, and the cattle population had dwindled noticeably. As far as the sheriff's department was concerned, Mayberry had become *Hill Street Blues*.

It was into this Mayberry existence, on January 20, 1966, that Laren Sims was born. It strangled her and choked her. She wanted to escape the atmosphere of pickup trucks, fishing trips, sipping beer under the power lines, and a mind-set in which the local high school football players were as famous as rock stars. But as a teenager, she had no idea how to get away. When she finally did figure out how to escape, it would come at a high price.

Laren would have to become another person. As her hometown metamorphosed, so would she. But her change would be much darker. She would become Elisa McNabney.

Those who remember Laren as a child say she often longed for more. Friends and relatives remember her as an animated young girl playing outside with her siblings, and her mother Jackie called Laren "a dreamer." But even then she apparently didn't fit into the country-living existence into which she was born. "She had so much to offer, but she got frustrated very easily," her mother said.

Like George Bailey in *It's a Wonderful Life,* she wanted to shake the dust of the town from her and see the world. The key difference between her and the decent, fictional George Bailey was that Laren couldn't accept anything less, and would do *anything* to get more.

What does it profit a man to gain the world and lose his soul? That ideal wasn't something that young Laren Sims would ever contemplate, let alone understand.

Her ideals were elsewhere.

"She never wanted to pay the bill when it came due," her father says of her.

A reasonable man of stature in the Brooksville area, Jesse Sims is the Mayberry ideal of fatherhood. His neighbors, business acquaintances, and family speak of his soft-spoken, yet disciplined nature and good sense of humor. He said he tried everything with his daughter Laren, but from an early age she seemed to be cut from a different cloth.

She wasn't easily satisfied, and didn't mix with her brother, Lorne, who was fifteen months older, or her brother, Jason, who was four years younger.

Even her greatest attributes eventually caused her nothing but pain. "Hell, half of her problem was she was so good-looking," her brother Jason says evenly. "She could shake her body at a guy and he'd come running like a puppy dog."

"Truth is, though, she never went after the real good-looking ones," her mother remembers.

Her father adds to this: "She liked to have control, it seemed."

Exercising control over her life was the watchword of Laren's existence. She didn't like it when her parents set her up on dates, and she didn't like anyone telling her what to do, most especially her mother and father.

"We tried," her mother says. "I don't want anyone to think that we didn't." Soft-spoken, like her husband, with a heavy-lined brow, when Jackie thinks of her daughter's missed opportunities in life, she invariably winces and sobs. A mature woman whose good looks can still be seen behind her graying hair and perennial smile, Jackie said her daughter's attitude became harder to control as she got older.

This attitude affected her in school, where she had disciplinary problems, and sometimes she skipped school entirely. Her teachers described her as moody and distant, as well as stubborn. Friends said she was outgoing, but rebellious. She could routinely find herself in problems of her own creation involving anyone in authority, lashing out against her parents, teachers, and even the police.

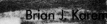

According to one friend at the time, Laren simply didn't care for "anyone telling her what to do about anything at any time."

Yet it appeared that Laren was able to handle the problems she encountered. Friends talk about her to this day in nearly reverential tones as they discuss how she could sweet-talk or con her way out of anything.

This proved to be beneficial to her family in at least one way: Jason said he got into less trouble than Laren did because as a younger sibling, he watched and learned what not to do from his older sister. He also remembered other, more typical encounters with his older sister. "I guess we beat the shit out of each other a couple of times when we were kids," he said with a grin. "You know, nothing too serious. Typical brother and sister stuff."

An outgoing, friendly sort with a perpetual grin on his face, Jason describes himself as the kind of guy who likes fishing and "watching a bobber better than driving in traffic." His sister was never like that. "She called it a simple life," he said. "And since she was drop-dead gorgeous and could turn heads, she was pretty sure she didn't have to live the life we live."

By the time she was a sophomore in high school, the young cheerleader who liked to spend time under the power lines out in the country with her friends, drinking and partying, thought she'd had enough of school. Her tenth grade class photo shows her with short-cropped hair and small earrings. Wearing eye shadow and a V-neck shirt with a collar, she looks nothing like the woman into which she would eventually evolve. Rather, she appears reserved and a bit shy. Her picture is opposite a page of three of her schoolmates and the caption, "These are the best of times." Many other pictures feature quotes from songs popular in the late 1970s and early 1980s, including "Dream On" by Aerosmith.

But by then Laren had decided she wasn't living in the best of times, and her behavior was an indication. She had already developed the conning attitudes that she would later be well known for.

One woman who remembers her as a teenager said she once watched Laren talk a police officer out of giving her a speeding ticket: "She was so smooth with him."

Another time, "She smiled and said, very much, you know, like an apology, that she had run a stop sign because she had to rush home because it was her time, you know, of the month, and the cop got all red and smiled and let her go."

Others who knew Laren as a teenager remembered her talking about leaving town and making it big. One of her school girlfriends recalls her saying she admired the saying, "Go west," although she didn't at the time know who she was quoting.

Her parents remember sessions of tough love and strife as they tried, first, to get Laren to finish school, and then later to get a steady job and prepare for some kind of future. It wasn't easy. "She got frustrated and tried to sell real estate, but couldn't," her father said. "Then she tried to sell insurance."

"She fought us constantly," her mother says through tears. "We loved her deeply, and that love never disappeared, but she was very strong-willed."

"Only she couldn't see that she was her own worst enemy," her father added. "Never could see that." She was a child who would "give you the answer you wanted to hear" when confronted, and she was constantly dreaming of better things. "She had the right dreams, but she didn't want to work to get them."

Her father tried to impose his will, reminding her that if she wanted to live in his house, then she had to live by his rules. In turn, she lied to him and her mother about "just about everything," he says.

When she began to get in trouble with the law for writing bad checks, her parents took her to a psychiatrist. "She was smarter than the psychiatrist," her father says flatly. Her IQ of 140 would appear to corroborate his assessment. But she used her intellect her own way, and to her own ends. "She was a habitual liar," Jesse Sims adds. "Someone that would just give you the answer you wanted to hear."

"She put her dad and I through a lot," her mother explains. "She was impatient and needed instant gratification. She just assumed people would believe her, and if they didn't, then she assumed she could talk her way out of her trouble."

She did this often, making excuses for being late or not showing up for appointments, and did it with a slickness that impressed those around her. Whether she was talking the police out of giving her a ticket, or a store manager out of prosecuting her for a bad check, or her parents out of being hard on her for sidestepping their rules, everyone who knew Laren at the time agreed she could talk herself out of any situation where there might be a confrontation.

She also had a love of the movies. "She could see her life as a movie. Absolutely," said a friend of hers from high school. "She talked about it a lot sometimes. But, she never really seemed to know how to make it happen for her. I think she just got bored and tired with living around here."

After skipping school, dropping out, not holding on to a job, and going through endless arguments and fights with siblings and parents, it looked as if Laren's life was never going to be what she wanted. But possessing a strong spirit and motivated to get what she wanted, she never gave up.

Everyone said about Laren that she wanted a lot out of life, and her friends say she wasn't finding it in her hometown from friends, family, or lovers.

"She looked restless usually," says one of her friends from those days. "All the guys were in love with her, but she didn't seem to have much of a use for any of them."

She was enamored of the glamorous life she saw in the movies and was drawn to the lifestyle in *The Great Gatsby*. But she especially admired the cunning of another big screen character based on real life. "She loved Faye Dunaway in *Bonnie and Clyde*," one of her high school friends said.

When she was eighteen, Laren finally grew so tired of hanging out at Louie's bowling alley, drinking beer, and running with the "popular crowd," she tried something different and got married to Scott Jordan, a local man close to her age who seemed to Laren different from the rest of her friends.

"I think she was trying to fit in," a high school acquaintance said of Laren's marriage experience. "I think she wanted to be like everybody else, but she couldn't pull it off." It didn't work out.

By the time she was twenty, she was divorced and had a daughter, Haylei. Later, she had a son, Cole, by a different man, Kirk Wilson, who was seventeen years older than she was. It was a minor scandal and her parents wouldn't talk too much about the specifics.

"Her relationships had a way of not working out," her father said.

It was only a matter of time before Laren would leave the small confines of Brooksville and venture out into the world and ultimately into her deadly dance with Larry McNabney.

That dance started, some would say in an appropriate manner, with a theft—a theft of Christmas presents, according to her parents. Afterward, her life would become a tome of ill fortune based on the foundation of that single crime, thereby answering the age-old question, "What happens to people who steal Christmas presents?"

In 1989, Laren had begun to date a series of what her brother called "losers." One man she dated was recently separated from his wife. "He wasn't that good-looking," her brother says, "but she never went for the good-looking guys. It was a control thing. He was a bad guy; insincere."

But who had control of whom? As it turns out, her boyfriend convinced Laren to go to his ex-wife's house—or she let him think so—and, of all things, steal the Christmas presents under the tree. He'd told her that the presents were really his and he wanted to give them to his kids. Later, she admitted to police, "I went to his ex-wife's house and took stuff out of her house that was what I thought was his, blah blah blah, you know, and then it was crazy . . . which you don't realize, and then you take that stuff and you sell it . . ."

Though she was apprehended, she later claimed she turned herself in two days after she stole the property. Her arrest record for grand theft is dated January 9, 1989. She was charged with burglary of a dwelling on March 22, 1989, and petty theft on that same day. She was also charged with dealing in stolen property.

After her arrest, Laren would never again flirt with the idea of working hard and waiting patiently for the things she wanted. It simply took too long.

But her arrest was a watershed event in her life for another reason. Afterward, she would not put herself in a position in which she allowed a man to dominate her. She would never place herself in a situation where a man could constrain her or impose his will over her. She had been permanently scarred. She would never lose control again.

As she saw it, she had given her love to a man, and he had used her. Young, romantic Laren Sims had suffered a broken heart from which she would not recover. She believed she'd suffered harshly for a crime from which her boyfriend got away free and clear. For this and other reasons, she became determined that in the future if anyone was going to suffer, it would not be her.

Without a previous criminal record, Laren was given

probation as a first offender. Then she bounced some checks. Her parents say the checks were for minor things, nothing more than groceries or other small ticket items. She got into additional trouble when she went to Tampa, violating her probation agreement so she could see a professional hockey game. As luck would have it, her probation officer attended the same game and saw her there.

As a probation violator, she was tossed in jail and ended up serving nine months. After her release, Laren declared she'd learned her lesson. "Anyone who goes to prison and does not learn their lesson deserves to go back. I am here my first time. I pray it is my last. I have learned," she wrote a clerk at the Hernando County Courthouse.

But Tom Hogan, the attorney her parents had arranged to help her, said she "had a real definite problem believing [her treatment by the judicial system] was fair."

Despite what she said about learning her lesson, after being released she quickly violated her probation again. "I got out of prison and didn't have any money," Laren told police. "I used somebody's credit card, one of my boss's credit cards or whatever." Justifying the theft by telling herself she needed the cash to support herself and her young daughter, she later told Haylei, "Don't steal, don't think just because somebody had something you don't have that you're entitled to it. That won't work."

Upon her release this time, she was forced to wear an ankle monitor as a condition for continued probation. "Everything she did was minor, but it all just snowballed," Hogan said.

On the face of it, it appeared to be a small infraction, and once again Laren had been the instrument of her own destruction. Apparently willing to take shortcuts to get what she wanted, and while seeming to have the best intentions, she still used seriously impaired judgment in making decisions. Some would call her actions "stupid stunts," while others would label them "criminal activity." Whatever it was, her attorney said most of it had its roots in a woman who, as she grew older, couldn't accept reality. "One of her many faults was that she just always tried to live beyond her means," Tom Hogan later said.

But it wasn't excessively malicious trouble, nor was it a violent crime. She wasn't bilking people for their life savings, she hadn't used a gun and hadn't tried to physically harm anyone at any point. Her parents, who balanced their love for their daughter with their desire to discipline her because of her criminal tendencies, never saw a violent side to Laren. "She was always very kind," her mother said. "I couldn't see her harming anybody like that."

Indeed, the only person really hurt by Laren was Laren. The Christmas presents were returned; the credit card scam had resulted in restitution. Bad checks had been made good, and everything else could have been okay.

But Laren didn't see it that way. When she got in trouble again because of her petty criminal activities, including being seen in Tampa at a hockey game by her parole officer, she chafed at the restrictions of her parents and the law like a dog whose collar was too tight.

She wanted financial security, and she wanted to travel. The larger world beckoned and she trembled with wanting it. She desired excitement and a challenge, and all she got in Brooksville were men whom she believed to be intellectually inferior to her, and a seemingly never-ending round of disciplinary actions from the local bumpkin law enforcement officers. She aspired to do more than hang out, or fish in the Gulf of Mexico, or hunt in the countryside, or live in a large log home in the middle of the woods with her parents. The town and her endless, petty bouts with the law convinced her that she had to leave. She was too smart, too restless, for the backwoods.

Laren was at a crossroads in the early months of 1993 when she found herself facing additional jail time after violating her parole by leaving the county without permission. She came to a decision then that would permanently change the course of her life. Often, she had been accused of shirking her responsibilities. She avoided being accountable for any of her misdeeds, and her father had accused her of being unable to pay the bill when it came due. When the bill came due for violating her parole, things would be no different.

She could stay and pay with more jail time, or could take off across the country. She decided to flee.

The reasons were many. She didn't want to embarrass her family anymore, and thought she was the black sheep of the family. Her father and mother were almost Norman Rockwell icons in Brooksville. She was the bad girl who couldn't help but feel that she didn't belong. She didn't know how to make things right, and wasn't entirely sure who she was or what she wanted. All she knew is that she wanted out.

That led to feelings of being trapped, and every time she thought about her inabilities to finish school or settle down or find the right guy, it only pushed against any feelings of loyalty to her family or staying in Brooksville.

Her intention to break out and get away was complicated by two things—actually, two people: her children. On the one hand, her five-year-old son Cole, who had cerebral palsy, would be a considerable liability for a woman on the run. His need for special education, special attention, and other special measures made him extremely high maintenance for Laren, despite the love she felt for him. She would have to spend most of her energy just taking care of herself, and she needed to travel light and quick. Logistically, Cole would be a nightmare.

She also had her seven-year-old daughter Haylei, who looked like Laren, had her quick wit, and Laren liked her. Not that she didn't like her son—she adored him. But Haylei fit into the game plan much better and could be an asset, and there would also be plenty of opportunity to be with her exclusively on the road. As smart as Haylei was and as self-sufficient as she seemed to be, even from a young age, Laren felt she could function as well with Haylei along. But most of all, Laren didn't want to leave town without her daughter. Her young daughter could provide needed companionship and love.

Whether she would take Haylei with her was a

tricky problem that kept her mind occupied and ultimately delayed her decision to leave Florida until she could work out the details. Many said Laren saw Haylei as a toy that she played with until she was bored, and then she would toss her aside. "I really felt sorry for Haylei," Tavia Williams, Larry McNabney's daughter, said. It was a sentiment echoed by everyone who ever met or knew Haylei after her mother fled Florida.

In fact, Laren did use Haylei for her own purposes when she had her around, and she did eventually discard her in the way many wealthy parents do—she sent Haylei to boarding schools.

As she contemplated leaving Florida during the last few weeks of 1992, Laren did not know where the road she planned to travel would take her, nor what it would mean to have a daughter by her side. She wondered how she would feed herself, much less the two of them, and how she would care for her daughter's material, social, educational, and other needs.

Given who Laren was, and what her shortcomings were, she did strive to meet her daughter's needs as best as she could. In fact, at times Haylei's needs helped fuel her mother's desires for greater wealth, more security, and a better living environment. Laren was no different, in that way, than any other mother. She simply believed that the ends always justified the means.

Besides the potential for hurting her son and her daughter by fleeing, Laren had other, more pressing problems. She knew she couldn't leave town as Laren

Sims—the police would be looking for her. So she pilfered the identity of a woman she had befriended during one of her jail terms: Elizabeth Barasch, an older woman who had been serving time for trafficking in cocaine. Laren had stumbled across her Social Security number and still remembered it. That number would be all she needed to assume the woman's identity and adapt it to her needs. First, however, she planned to shorten the name a bit. Elizabeth became Elisa.

With an identity secured, Laren begged, borrowed, and apparently stole enough money to get out of town. This left her with the lingering problem of what to do with her two children. Cole was already living with his father, so it was a simple matter for Laren to run away from both of them—despite her strong feelings for her son.

So, it was down to Haylei. It always boiled down to Haylei. It was Haylei whom Laren thought about constantly. Ultimately, living without her daughter was too much for her, so she had to take Haylei.

In 1992, at the age of seven, Haylei Sims-Jordan was photographed by the *Tampa Tribune* riding a merry-go-round in Ruskin, Florida. A happy-go-lucky child captured for posterity in a human-interest moment, according to the *Sacramento Bee*. But within months she would be nowhere near the state of Florida. She'd be on the lam with her mother.

"She walked into my bedroom one night and told me she was going away," her daughter says. "She asked me if I wanted to go with her, and of course I did. She was my mother. I loved her very much. And I asked about Cole"—her half brother—"and she told me he couldn't go with us because of his illness."

"It's just gonna be me and you now," her mother whispered to her while Haylei was in bed.

On March 23, 1993, facing more jail time, depressed, lonely, and feeling cornered, Laren decided to cut her ties, literally and figuratively, with the past she couldn't stand for a lifestyle and possibilities she couldn't at that point begin to fathom. Cutting off the ankle monitor that linked her to her parole officer and the rest of the criminal justice system made her feel free. Exhilarated, yet with great trepidation, she gathered up her young daughter and headed west.

Haylei had hoped her mom would take her to New York. She loved the thought of going to the city that never sleeps, but Laren had other plans. She was going to follow famed newspaper editor Horace Greeley's advice and head west, seeking fame and fortune while living on the lam by any means available to a young, single, fugitive mother with a young daughter.

Her parents wouldn't hear from her for nearly ten years.

3

A Real Sharp Chick

Laren Sims always had the ability to land on her feet.
Time and again, with the odds against her, she was able
to get the money she needed, or the help, or the house,
or the car, or whatever it was she wanted. It was a remarkable ability that earned her the nickname of the
"Chameleon" in her hometown paper after one of her
arrests. While she was free she was merely thought of
as smart and good-looking. For those who knew her
well, however, she was also considered dangerous.

She carried herself in a classy manner. She didn't
dress in sleazy clothes, nor did she accentuate her
voluptuous figure. Hers was a demeanor cultivated by
the good upbringing of her parents and she used it to
help take the shortcuts to the riches she desired. When
she left Florida, her innate intelligence, outgoing nature, and inner drive all served her well. It seemed she
could talk anyone into anything, and as one friend later
said of her, she never went on a job interview without

landing the job. Her good looks helped her find young men eager to assist her, and her sly intelligence enabled her to con her way into any environment in which she felt comfortable.

It was a game Laren loved to play, and she played it masterfully. For her, it was fun to outsmart those who thought they were smarter than others. It was partly payback for what she'd gone through, and it was also a thrill—to put one over on people who thought they couldn't be fooled. And it was the only game she knew in order to survive, to put bread on the table, to thrive. Cornered in a box of her own construction, her life became a virtuoso performance of cunning and conning in which she was always the lead solo player in the orchestra. And, since Laren saw her life as a movie, she was always writing, rewriting, and tweaking her self-image in the film inside her head.

Her transformation began in Las Vegas, a town where people reinvent themselves like others change their underwear. By early 1993 she and Haylei had moved into an apartment complex on the city's north side. Laren had renamed herself Elisa Barasch by then while her daughter remained Haylei Sims Jordan, with her father's last name. From the beginning of Laren's flight from prosecution and her past, she struggled hard to make things as normal as possible for her daughter, which was why Haylei kept her name—so she could be secure in her identity. Laren also sent her to private schools, in an attempt to shelter her from some of the more unsavory elements of her own daily existence, like the cons and the theft in which she was involved.

It didn't always work. Some of Elisa definitely rubbed off on her daughter. Hairdressers who worked on Elisa in Nevada and California recalled that even as a very young girl, Haylei was prone to exaggerations and lies, much like her mother. "She would lie about stupid stuff that didn't make any sense," one hairdresser said. "She'd lie about what she had for lunch."

Haylei knew of some of her mother's deceptions, such as her different aliases, but the girl believed her mother was on the run because of a child custody battle involving her father. Perhaps she wanted to believe it. Haylei said she always "wanted to protect my mom" and that they were "partners in crime."

In fact, no one knew to what extent they were partners, given the fact that Elisa worked hard to keep Haylei at arm's length during critical times, so her daughter wouldn't be implicated in her crimes and could live without fear of her mother's past. "Her love for her daughter at least seemed genuine," says one of her acquaintances from that period in her life.

Meanwhile, Elisa was afraid of being returned to Florida. She'd violated her parole, after all. This fear dominated much of what she did during her years on the lam. But it wasn't as big a problem as she thought. She was not a master criminal, and back in Florida, while bench warrants were eventually issued for her felonious flight from the state, Laren Sims was not high enough on anyone's most wanted list, certainly not enough to warrant a manhunt. To the state of Florida, she was merely one of thousands of low-level criminals avoiding the law. Stolen credit cards, stolen

Christmas presents, and a couple of parole violations made her of interest, but in Florida, a state that Fox television staff members often joke helps keep *America's Most Wanted* on the air, no bounty hunter was going to come busting down her door, nor would a TV program be interested in highlighting her criminal flight from the law—not yet, at least.

Eventually, a few months after they settled down in Las Vegas, Elisa's life began to take on some shades of normalcy. When she and Haylei first moved into Green Valley, a new upscale neighborhood at the time, they had a nice apartment but no furniture. It was Elisa's life in a nutshell: pretty on the outside and empty on the inside.

Food, shelter, and clothing were problematic until Elisa found work managing a chiropractor's office. Clients there remember her as charming, outgoing, and easy to get along with, skills she'd been honing in Brooksville. In Las Vegas, she was sharpening them to a lethal edge.

Her cheery manner, long legs, big smile, pretty face, and big breasts made her an attraction and distraction for those in the office. Her ability to blend with others using charm, flattery, and deceit made her a disaster just waiting to happen to some poor unfortunate who stumbled across her path.

His name was Ken Redelsperger.

Ken had just started his own insurance agency, but he was hardly the deskbound type. Rather, he was an active outdoors man in his mid-thirties. He was into Motocross, snow and water skiing, fishing, camping, and the like, and while he had dated a variety of girls, none seemed as enamored of the rugged, outdoor life as he himself was. After a motorcycle accident in 1993, he went to the chiropractor's office to have his back injuries treated. From then on, things were never the same for him.

Elisa immediately caught Ken's eye, and she also felt an attraction to Ken. It probably began innocently enough, a casual flirtation or a glance. At some point, her survival instincts would have taken over. She had the ability to size people up almost immediately and understand how she could use them to further her own ends. Even had she wanted to exercise any control in the matter, she probably would have been set in a course of action.

Ken didn't see it coming, and later said he never had a chance. He was infatuated with her, and what began as a friendship evolved into something more intimate. From the moment he met her, he found her satisfying in many ways. "She was a real sharp chick," he says. "It was refreshing to see someone so blunt and seemingly honest. She had a way about her. She just said, 'Hey, I like you. Let's go out.'"

He asked Elisa and Haylei to go fishing with him because he could see that Elisa "loved her daughter a lot." He found that an attractive quality because he had always wanted a family. It seemed a perfect fit; conveniently, Ken had found a ready-made family.

But other things about his new girlfriend bothered Ken. The first time he went to Elisa's apartment, he found it empty; there was no furniture at all. Both mother and daughter apparently slept on a pallet in the bedroom, in which there was only the barest of wardrobes and other accessories. What little clothes were in the apartment were stacked neatly on the floor or hanging in a bedroom closet.

Ken found it incongruous with the lifestyle he expected of someone living in that upscale neighborhood. Elisa explained the lack of furniture by saying that her parents had repossessed it from her because she had moved to Las Vegas against their will. In fact, they probably would have objected to her living in Vegas, since she was violating parole and was a wanted fugitive who'd fled across state lines on a minor offense.

But it was pure fantasy that they would have confiscated her furniture, had she had any furniture they could have taken. Ken suspected as much when she told him her story, because he noticed "there were no marks in the carpet to show there'd ever been any furniture in the house." But he didn't say anything. "I just kind of overlooked it," he says.

Elisa, expanding on her fiction, told him she would soon be the recipient of an inheritance from her grandparents—in either Cuba or Puerto Rico—and so her fortunes would soon change. As he stood in the empty apartment and listened to her tell this incredible story, Ken overlooked his suspicions a second time, though he was skeptical of the claims. He was blinded by Elisa's attractiveness and her convincing manner.

It was rumored by at least one coworker that she was dating her boss, the chiropractor, but if so, it did not interfere with her seeing Ken more and more. If she had any boyfriend at all while living in Las Vegas for the short time before she met Ken, after she met Ken, it seemed he was the sole recipient of her charm and focus.

Not long after meeting Elisa, he invited her and Haylei to move into his big three-bedroom house. A bachelor for many years, Ken enjoyed the thought of spending time with them, and to this day he speaks about Elisa and Haylei with mixed emotions. He knew she wasn't what she claimed to be, but still enjoyed himself, and loved the time he spent teaching Haylei how to ride Motocross and ski. He fell in love with both of them, he confides now, and was determined to be a devoted lover to Elisa and father to Haylei.

He was to find out what Elisa was all about shortly after she moved in with him.

One night while they were watching television, Elisa told Ken that she felt guilty about not paying any bills, and that she wanted the opportunity to pull her weight. Glancing toward a counter in another room, Ken said there were some minor bills there, and if she wanted to, she could pay one or more. In truth, the bills didn't concern him. He was being kind to her. But Elisa had abandoned the notion that acts of kindness were based on love or friendship. In Florida she had given her heart to a man who feigned kindness, and it had led her to jail time and a life on the run. So now she met Ken's gestures of kindness in a far more calculating manner.

Inspecting the bills, she found a credit card in Ken's name. It didn't have much of a limit, but Elisa put it to good use without Ken's knowledge—until he got the bill about a month later. They hadn't been together as a couple for long when he came to realize that his involvement with her could mean a substantial dent in his wallet. Having just started the insurance agency, he didn't want to incur debts, so he asked her to move out.

She did, for a few brief weeks, moving with Haylei back to the threadbare apartment. She continued to see Ken, and he eventually let her back into his life and his house. No doubt she was taken by his up-and-coming business, his potential—not only as a spouse, but as a revenue stream.

They continued their relationship for nearly two years before finally deciding to get married in 1994. Despite his past problems with her financial free-handed nature, Ken looked forward to the marriage. But while he now thought he knew her, for better or worse, he still didn't even know her real name, and he had no idea she was a parole violator and a fugitive from Florida.

"I don't remember ever hearing that name," Ken would later tell the *Sacramento Bee*, referring to the name Laren Sims. "And I never saw her check in with a parole officer or anything."

They stayed married for just six months.

"Everything I saw before, I saw again. She didn't change," he explained. "I loved her, and I don't know what her true feelings for me were. Still don't know."

Ken put a lot into the relationship, but, not surprisingly, said he sometimes felt he wasn't getting out what he put into it. There were times when he found his young, attractive wife secretive and elusive. She wouldn't always tell him where she had been after going out for an afternoon. And there was also the continued onslaught of bills as Elisa spent wildly.

"She didn't always make it easy on me, that's for sure," he now says matter-of-factly.

But she didn't seem to be teetering on the edge, as she later was. "She wasn't into drugs or anything more than a little pot," he explained. "She was pretty well put together, I thought."

Part of that could be attributed to who Ken was. He had no attraction to the darker side of living that Elisa could feed and prey on. He didn't flirt with abusing narcotics and he didn't have a drinking problem. He was clean living, and consequently so was Elisa. Had she been anything but what he wanted, she knew he wouldn't keep her around. And the "Chameleon" knew how to adapt to her surroundings.

Elisa had embedded herself in Ken's life by taking on the role that she figured he wanted most: a good lover, a camping partner, a fishing pal, a nurse who took care of him when he was injured, and a skiing buddy who looked great in a bikini or in snow boots. What more could a man ask?

Her obvious assets would make many a man overlook something as trivial as his wallet—at least until it became problematic to look the other way.

Even with the strife she brought, Ken has fond memories of his time with Elisa. "We had a lot of fun together," he says. "Haylei laughed a lot and so did her mother. There was never any pressure, and I thought we were enjoying ourselves."

She had ingrained herself in Ken's family too, becoming a fond companion of Ken's grandmother, whom he loved very much. And his grandmother grew to be as enamored of the beautiful young lady and her attractive young daughter as Ken was. Even so, Ken would try to break free of her orbit soon after they married.

"I knew what she was, and I fell in love with her anyway," he says. "She was a real bright chick, but she focused her energy in the wrong direction. Almost everything she said to me was a lie. I think the only thing she told me that was true was that her parents were good."

But they weren't either Cuban or Puerto Rican refugees, as Elisa claimed to different people at different times. Jesse and his wife Jackie were still living in the country acreage outside of Brooksville, Florida, that had been their home for many years. Jesse, one of just forty-seven graduates in 1960 from the county's high school, was a local boy born in the Brooksville area. Elisa had woven such a thick fabric of lies for Ken that it was almost impenetrable.

"We were together for almost two years, but only married six months. The hardest thing I ever had to do was divorce her. I loved her and I loved Haylei."

They did a lot of things together, and Ken, who'd never fathered a child himself, looked upon Haylei as his daughter. One Saturday he taught her to ride dirt bikes. The next day she was in a Motocross race, and Ken was never prouder. "She was a smart girl," he says. "Very protective of her mother, but otherwise a real intelligent, beautiful girl."

Another time, the three of them took a vacation together on the beach. Mother and daughter rented horses and rode along the beach, a passion they both shared. Ken, usually the adventurer, sat and watched, amused and enamored of both his stepdaughter and his wife. It was a moment of innocent fun that he remembers fondly. But in the scheme of things, it was a joyous rarity.

Eventually, Ken came to realize that his love for Elisa wasn't a healthy thing. She lied constantly and connived to get the money to buy anything and everything she wanted. "She was just sucking me in," he explained. A money vacuum that was never turned off, she had an insatiable appetite for the finest things in life, and Ken couldn't feed her appetite without putting himself and his new business in jeopardy, which was something his survival instincts wouldn't allow.

Meanwhile, her employer had also become unable to feed Elisa's desires. She found the chiropractor's office stuffy and stifling. It didn't bring in enough money, it was unsatisfying to the ego and the intellect, and she saw it as a dead end. She needed more—much more.

Ultimately, Elisa's needs and weaknesses began to work on Ken, especially when she lied and he felt compelled to cover for her. "You know, I began to feel bad about myself," he says. "I'd cover her on just the smallest, stupidest things and feel bad about it later. I was just at the point where I had my insurance agency and I could see that she was going to threaten it, and I couldn't let her sink me no matter how much I loved her."

As an example of how she drew him into her world of deception, Ken recounts the time his Labrador gave birth. He sold a puppy to a new neighbor he didn't know too well. About a month later Elisa went over to take care of the puppy while the neighbors were away, and after the visit, the puppy wasn't at the home anymore.

Ken isn't sure what happened to it. "Maybe she gave it to someone else she was smoothing over," he said.

She told the neighbors the dog got lost, and didn't give anything but the sketchiest of details. The neighbors didn't buy the story, and Ken backed her up. Still, when pressed, he felt guilty about what had happened and gave back the money the neighbors had paid for the dog.

"Just stupid things," Ken says. "She was so bright, but did some of the stupidest things. What a waste."

Shortly after they were married, Haylei wrote a letter to her brother Cole back in Florida. She asked him how he was doing, and said their mom had finally met a nice guy named Ken and that she herself was happy because she finally had a dad.

Haylei had given the note to her mother to mail home to Florida. It sat in a nightstand for months, and when Elisa and Haylei had moved out, Ken found it.

For her part, Elisa finally recognized Ken's fear that she was going to drag him into financial ruin. Having left the chiropractor's office, she began work answering phones and doing general secretarial work for an attorney specializing in handling bankruptcies. Then, one day, answering an ad for a secretary, Elisa found herself at the Las Vegas law offices of Larry McNabney.

Another role of the dice and another chance encounter was about to change her life and the lives of others. Larry McNabney would never be the same.

From the beginning, it was an environment in which Elisa felt comfortable. She had learned a lot in her last job, and now found herself better at the snarling vicissitudes of the law than most lawyers. Spinning the truth, within legal limits, is not only accepted, but those lawyers who do well at it are often among the richest. Elisa wasn't bound by legal ethics or limits, but found herself loving work in a law firm. Her personal experience with the law gave her a smattering of legal knowledge that was enough to impress Larry McNabney, who was an extremely well-known criminal defense and personal injury attorney when they met.

Ken was not distressed by Elisa's sudden and growing infatuation with her employer, for by now he was aware of his dwindling finances and trying desperately to get Elisa out of his life and house. So in fact he was glad to see Elisa out with someone else. "I actually thought, thank God, Larry is going to take her off my hands," he says.

When he eventually broke up with her, Ken still felt responsible for Haylei, and so after the divorce, Elisa and Haylei continued to live with him. It was an odd arrangement.

Two months after she went to work for Larry, Ken saw her with a new, black, supercharged Jaguar. He also witnessed another metamorphosis in Elisa. She had gone from being the earth-mother, outdoors type to a sophisticated legal secretary adept at running Larry's life, setting up appointments, and speaking with jet setters.

"She was home one day and called to put a deposit on a Learjet that Larry wanted to charter so she and Larry could travel together," he recalls.

Clearly, the chameleon in Laren/Elisa was changing its appearance.

Haylei stayed home with Ken, and he provided the care and comfort of a father as Elisa went out of town with Larry. It was a situation that occurred on several occasions. Usually, Larry and Elisa would disappear for a weekend before she came back.

In late 1995, Ken was scheduled to go on a snowmobile trip for a week and couldn't watch Haylei. Elisa, already in Reno with Larry, said that was fine and asked him to take Haylei to the airport and put her on a flight to Reno, where her daughter would join her and her new boyfriend. Ken did it, leaving Haylei with little more than a weekend's worth of clothing. After all, Elisa had said she'd be back early in the week. "I still feel guilty about not packing more for her that weekend," Ken says now.

The reason is simple to understand, for after Ken dropped off Haylei, he never saw her again.

When he returned to Las Vegas after his trip, Elisa contacted Ken to let him know she and her daughter wouldn't be coming back. She'd found better arrangements with Larry McNabney.

Despite the financial difficulties he'd had with Elisa, and his relief that he would no longer have to put up with those problems, Ken was crestfallen. He genuinely cared for both of them, and felt guilty that nine-year-old Haylei had left him without even a suitcase full of clothes. He told Elisa to come and get their stuff, including photos of their time together, other memorabilia, and their clothes, but Elisa had cut herself off from her past once again.

Ken was gone from her life. She didn't want the pictures.

Larry McNabney was now at center stage, and he looked to be able to provide her, materially, with everything she wanted. He was a rich lawyer who had social connections that made Ken's situation seem pale in comparison.

It was up and on to bigger and brighter things for Laren Sims/Elisa Barasch Redelsperger.

For Ken, it was an eye-opener he still hasn't entirely come to grips with. A few weeks after Elisa left, he again silently thanked Larry for taking her off his hands, then packed all of Elisa's and Haylei's personal possessions into his car and drove them to Larry McNabney's office, where he left them in the lobby for Elisa to retrieve.

"She'd call me once or twice a year after that to tell me she loved me," Ken says.

Thinking of that and what ultimately happened to Larry McNabney makes him shudder. Elisa had bilked Ken for around $30,000. He got off lucky compared to Larry, and he knows it.

"I've thought about that since Larry died, and I can't make any sense of it," he says. "But it was hard to make sense of anything she said. She had a different story for each different occasion and each different person."

After Elisa left him and was living with Larry McNabney, she told Ken a new story. Perhaps she was scared he might run into Larry, talk to him, and hear new, contradictory things that might be a threat to her. "After we split up, she came to me and told me she was really on the run from the cops," Ken says. "She'd been busted for coke and the cops were making her snitch on dealers and she'd gotten tired of the hard life of looking at pictures of dead drug dealers. She just needed time, she said."

Like other stories Laren would tell during the years, the story of Elisa Barasch the unwilling snitch had a grain of truth to it, but otherwise it was a fabrication designed to buy her some time while she moved on to her next host.

Larry McNabney, like everyone else, had no idea what he was getting into. Larry and Elisa/Laren were married in early 1996. It was her second marriage in a year and the third in the last ten years. It was his fifth in the last twenty-five.

It was the last for both of them.

4

Think Ink!

Those who knew Larry McNabney the best say that he was a consummate professional. He once wanted to get rid of a secretary because he didn't like typographical errors she made in sending out his correspondence. "That reflects on my name and my credibility," he explained. He was a neat freak who wouldn't leave an unclean dish in the sink. He was also well known for his intolerance of liars, and admonished his children often about telling lies.

Considering all this, it is amazing that he let Elisa into his life. She was a woman who never much cared or worried about any of the things Larry considered important.

"Larry once told me he was drawn to the 'dark side' and that he couldn't help it," his longtime live-in love Cheryl Tangen says. Larry had certain appetites for edgy and questionable behavior that Cheryl said he rarely fed.

He met the dark side incarnate in Laren Sims/Elisa Barasch Redelsperger.

Meeting Larry McNabney was another seemingly random event in Elisa's haphazard life. She picked up a newspaper one day, looking for a job, and saw an advertisement for a position in his law firm. Larry was the rugged, tall, red-haired, good-looking personal injury lawyer who did his own commercials and could be seen on local billboards. In the television ads, he always wore a cowboy hat while sitting on a horse in the mountains. "Call me," he said.

She did.

Of course, knowing Elisa's nature, it could well be that her meeting Larry was not as haphazard or simple as it seemed. As police later speculated, she might have wanted to meet the local celebrity lawyer who was known by his friends to have an abundance of good times and a good deal of money. But whether by chance or design, after they began dating, Elisa relished in Larry's celebrity.

"Isn't my husband handsome?" she later wrote on a snapshot she had taken of Larry standing in front of one of his billboards. Certainly that was an attraction for her. The man on the small screen would fit a material need she was always looking to fulfill, as his Rolodex would help fill a social need she seemed to have.

As usual, after a quick interview, she got the job. She had applied for it under the name of Elisa Barasch Redelsperger, once again using the Social Security number and name she'd stolen from the inmate back in Florida, but this time along with her ex-husband's last name. It was a convenient cover, and it worked for more than two years. Her new employer, doing only the most cursory of background checks—if any at all—not only hired her quickly, but seemed to have immediately become smitten with her.

"You've got to meet this new secretary I just hired," Larry told his stepdaughter Tavia. "She's smart as a whip."

Tavia was a young blond who had grown close to Larry when her mother, JoDee, married him. She was surprised that her stepfather had become so taken with his new secretary so quickly. "You know, one day, my dad came to me with a big smile, looking different," she says. "He said, you're gonna like this new secretary I hired. She's pretty, she's smart and nice, and she knows how to run things, so I don't have to. She's great."

Indeed, Elisa quickly graduated from the secretarial position to become an office manager, running the firm.

Laurence William McNabney was born less than a week before Christmas, on December 19, 1948. By definition, he was one of the millions of post-WWII baby boomers who came of age listening to the Beatles, the Rolling Stones, experiencing the Summer of Love and smoking marijuana. But in fact he was not characteristic of that stereotype of his generation. As a young man, Larry was known to sport an Afro, but he was never a hippie. He always dressed "very dapper," according to his friends, and was studious and sometimes reserved. He was also a very serious student. Some say he could be downright shy.

It seemed incongruous, but Larry was also a ladies' man and never lacked for female companionship. He was a raconteur who would hold court with friends and acquaintances, leading them in laughter and fun. Part of the irreverence of his generation was seen in Larry's gregarious and outgoing nature, and in his cutting humor and his alcohol abuse. Tavia said alcohol was the lubricant that enabled him to ease himself into social settings and hold court. It's what enabled him to be the apparent happy-go-lucky party animal, when otherwise he would have been shy and reserved. But in his later years, Larry became more readily identifiable with another icon of his era: the Marlboro man.

One thing he had in common with his fifth wife, Laren Sims/Elisa Barasch Redelsperger, was the ability to recreate himself numerous times. As a young lawyer he was described as "smooth" and "cosmopolitan," sometimes referred to as the man "with a twinkle in his eye."

"Larry was probably the smartest, quickest lawyer I've ever been around. He was a magic man," said Air Force Major General Ron Bath, Larry McNabney's law partner for nearly eight years and who would eventually become head of strategic planning at the Pentagon.

"He was faster on his feet drunk than most people were sober," Bath says.

They got to know each other in law school. Bath was a few years older than Larry, but they were contemporaries because Bath had taken a few years off for Air Force service. "There was nobody better than Larry when he was hitting on all eight cylinders. He was a charmer," Bath recalls.

However, the charmer did not lead a charmed life. He knew tragedy well. In 1970, Larry's older brother, Jim, came home from Vietnam a damaged man. Like others scarred from the war, he got heavily into drugs and suffered a fatal overdose in August of that year. Then, three months later, shortly after Thanksgiving, Larry's father committed suicide. Those who knew the family say that Jim's death inspired his father's suicide.

JoDee Bebout, Larry's second wife—Tavia's mother—says he recovered from these tragedies and didn't try to hide from them. "He accepted death," she says.

Longtime girlfriend Cheryl Tangen, who dated Larry for years before he met Elisa, says, "He wouldn't hide his tears. That's one of the things that drew me to him."

Despite his early heartbreaks from the loss of his father and brother—or perhaps because of them—General Bath remembers Larry as one of the most outgoing people he'd ever met. "We were exact opposites, which perhaps is why our partnership worked so well together," he explains. "He was smooth and polished and had more presence. You couldn't be around him without being captivated by him. He was so damn likable. He was a magic man in winning people over and getting people to like him. I was this very conservative, quiet guy, and he was this flamboyant, high profile guy."

Friends from Larry's high school days also remember a happy, outgoing boy who "liked to have fun." In 1966 he graduated from Reno High School, and four years later picked up his bachelor's degree from the

University of Nevada, Reno. It was 1970, the year his father and brother died, and the year of Kent State. It was an unsettled time in American history, which drew college students by the thousands out onto their campuses in protest.

Larry's life was as tumultuous as the times. Friends in college remember him as a focused student when he wanted to be, and a party boy when the mood struck him. Some who knew him said he was mercurial, while others said he was a "kind of savant" and could get decent grades at will. One woman who knew him in college, however, said it was no big secret why Larry made the dean's list and constantly got good grades. He studied long and hard.

The unsettled times in which he was living awakened Larry's social conscience. It might have influenced his interest in law. He enrolled at the University of Pacific's McGeorge School of Law and applied himself to the work. For the first time, he had a goal in life. It was a nebulous one, but it could be summed up by what he told a former girlfriend: "I want to help people."

Other friends and acquaintances of his at the time disagree. They say he was interested in law merely for the money and prestige. It's possible, of course. He had grown up in an upper-middle-class environment, after all, and always had nice things.

"That's not to say that he didn't want to help people," JoDee Bebout, Larry's second wife, says opining that both altruism and self-interest motivated Larry to take up law. "He always had a good heart and liked to help people down on their luck."

His daughter, Tavia, says it was a lifelong habit. "He so admired people who worked hard with their hands and people who were less fortunate. He'd give them the shirt off of his back."

Cheryl Tangen described a similar man. "No one is better than anyone else," she says Larry told her.

When he graduated from law school in 1974, Larry and his future partner, Ron Bath, clerked together for a brief time for a deputy public defender in Washoe County, Nevada. The office, according to many there, was a confluence of intellect and talent whose pinnacle was personified in Larry McNabney. Besides Bath, the group of men who found themselves in the public defender's office in the mid-seventies went on to gain respect as politicians, judges, and attorneys.

"We've all done okay," Bath says. "At the time, we were all young, big stud guys ready to set the world on fire. And the public defender's office had been plagued by guys who didn't want to fight, and suddenly there we were, ready to try anything."

They all enjoyed fighting the system, and this too was part of the post-Vietnam/Watergate era in which they found themselves working as young lawyers. But romantic battles can be fought only so long before economic realities intrude. As fond as they were of fighting the good fight, the men eventually found themselves drained by the work. They would struggle to get on top of one case, only to find as many as ten others waiting for them. It was hard to give each case the attention it needed while making little money, and Larry and Ron soon found themselves ready for something else.

In 1977, about the time Laren Sims was beginning to negotiate puberty, Larry and Ron decided to partner their own law firm. Together, they purchased a mansion from an estate and made it their office. It was an office they came to love. "It was a beautiful old colonial house," Bath recalls. "We personally spent every night from May to October that year refurbishing the place. We wallpapered, painted, and we did the plumbing, even the electrical work, everything. It was a magic time for a couple of brand-new lawyers. We'd work in the court all day long and go and change clothes and then work in the house all night."

When the two opened their law firm, Larry was also working on his second marriage and had adopted his wife's daughter from her first marriage. He grew to love Tavia, and together with his own son and daughter, Joe and Cristin, he had a seemingly perfect family.

"His son was little Joey to us," recalls one of his friends from that time. "And his dad just loved him. He absolutely adored his children."

Barbara, Ron Bath's wife, and JoDee, Larry's wife at the time, also helped out in the office when they got a chance, and soon were socializing together, sharing a lifestyle as the two young, promising lawyers began a partnership that clicked from the very beginning. The only problem was more of a joke than anything else: what to call their firm? "Larry wanted to call it 'McNabney and Bath,' and Ron wanted to call it 'Bath and McNabney,'" JoDee said. "I mean it got spirited, but it was all in fun."

Finally, they decided to settle on alphabetical order, and so the partnership became "Bath and McNabney."

The pair worked together by day and hung out with each other by night, and meanwhile became rising stars on the local legal scene, gaining a reputation by taking on lucrative as well as high-profile cases.

"We got a reputation for taking on big-time cases and going to the wall with them," Bath explains. And, as always, Larry was ready to take advantage of a case. "He had a great line: 'Think Ink.' He always said, whether it was good or bad, it was always good to get ink."

In pursuit of his cases, and the ink, Larry did some "amazing things," his ex-partner remembers. His presentation in court could be flamboyant, but was always professional. According to those who knew him, he could get to the emotional core of a case and tweak it as few others could. A quiet man when by himself, his friends remembered Larry's flamboyance in the courtroom as standing in stark contrast to his otherwise quiet demeanor.

"In court he commanded attention," remembers a close friend. "He could be boisterous, but always had a twinkle in his eye. You couldn't not like him."

Larry seemed to grow into his job in the courtroom, taking it over as he had done with everything else in his life in which he had applied himself. Once, he even got involved in a murder case in which he got a psychic to testify. It got him attention. It helped the case.

On another case, Larry represented more than a dozen parents in their fight against a day care center accused of abusing some of its children. That case became so well known in the Southwest, some thought Larry would never have to work again, but they didn't know Larry McNabney.

He had made some money, had seen a good time, and worked his butt off. "He could've been President if he wanted to," his ex-partner says.

But Larry had at least one fatal flaw, or at least a common one. He liked to drink, and it occasionally interfered with his life. One of his favorite sayings, according to Ron Bath, was, "You can't put a price on a good time." Perhaps you can't, but after a while all the good times started taking a toll on their partnership.

"Larry could make money. But if he brought in a dollar, he'd spend a dollar thirty," a friend of his recalls.

He had acquired a taste for the high life, and while his friends and partner loved his flamboyance, it was a double-edged sword. Ron could drive a pickup to work and Larry a used lemon yellow Porsche, and it was okay. But the drinking and carousing and many friendships with women eventually led him to go through four wives before his fifth marriage to Laren Sims/Elisa Redelsperger.

Many of those wives recall similar stories of Larry being upbeat at some times and "darkly intense" at others.

"You don't go through what Larry went through in his life with his father and brother and not be affected," recalls Ron. "I'm sure that was a factor."

Ron covered for him for a while; after all, as Ron said, Larry drunk was still better than most people sober. But it was tough on Ron, a straight arrow who did not share Larry's flamboyant lifestyle. The partners never ended up shouting at each other, and it never became so difficult that Ron lost respect for Larry. But after a few years it became hard to keep their partnership together.

Ron decided he had to speak to Larry.

"He got so bad drinking that he and I had a long talk and then he checked himself into a rehab center." JoDee had sanctioned the rehab trip as well, and had talked him into getting some help for his drinking, which was starting to affect his home life as well.

The combination of his law partner and his wife talking to him apparently brought him back from the dark side, because, after rehab in the early 1980s, Larry applied himself with vigor. He stopped drinking and got back into shape. He had always been a man who cared about his appearance. A bit of a control freak who abhorred anything out of place, he became even more meticulous in his care for himself after he got out of rehab. "He was the type of guy whose every hair had to be in place," his ex-wife JoDee said. "He cared very much for his appearance."

His daughter said this care for grooming extended to other things as well. "I tell you what I remember," Tavia says. "My dad would come home from work every night and fix dinner for my mom. Dad loved to cook. But Dad never went to bed with a dirty dish in the sink. Ever, ever, ever. I lived with him longer than any woman in his life, and that just wasn't in him."

JoDee said she got the "fingertip" test over the top of the refrigerator more than once. "He liked things clean, but he wasn't mean about it. I'll tell you this, because of him I came to appreciate the finer things in life."

In fact, Larry himself began to appreciate things anew after he came out of rehab. "He came out and was just a completely new person," Bath recalls. "He got himself into incredible condition and ran the New York marathon. If he put his mind to it, he could do anything."

It was an attitude that always succeeded in attracting women, even if Larry didn't party as he had before he went to rehab. "He just had a smile that women loved," says a former law clerk. "He was a good-looking guy, but it was that smile. He always had women just hanging around him—beautiful women. I mean really beautiful women."

His charming manner, his looks, his demeanor, everything about him made Larry very attractive to Elisa Barasch Redelsperger.

"He had a real rapier wit about him. Very dry," an ex-client says of him.

Perhaps that was the initial attraction between Larry and Elisa. They both had the ability to light up a room with their smiles, poke fun, be playful and tease. Elisa was by every account more comfortable in public than Larry, but even so, they shared a common ground in their humor.

"He got this little twinkle in his eye, like the cat who ate the canary," JoDee Bebout says.

"My dad could always make you laugh," Tavia says. "Sometimes he'd kid you and you wouldn't know it, and then he'd look at you and you'd know."

Those who befriended him said that while he could be sarcastic, he was always charming and very sophisticated.

In 1985, Ron ejected out of an F-4, broke his back, and had to retrain on the jets he loved to fly for the Air Force. The agonizing and intense physical rehabilitation after the accident consumed most of Ron's time. The partnership withered on the vine as a result.

Meanwhile, that same year, Larry, seeing the writing on the wall, became a special deputy district attorney and worked in the D.A.'s office for a while. The next year, he found a new gig. He became a federally appointed defense attorney in the "Company" case, which proved to be the longest federal drug trial in U.S. history. It was high profile, intense, and in the full glare of the media for months. Larry drank it up and enjoyed the challenge, the notoriety, and the money as he engineered and helped control a defense team.

Afterward, he didn't want to do much anymore. With the money he'd made and the reputation he earned, he abruptly retired. But the retirement wouldn't last very long. Larry was too restless, and since he liked to spend money, he needed to make it.

In just three years he found himself back in Reno, opening a personal injury practice at the end of the 1980s. If managed well, this can be a very lucrative specialty for a lawyer. Larry, excelling at everything he did, as usual, began to do so well that he opened offices in Las Vegas and Elko, Nevada, as well as Sacramento, California.

By then, with his marriage to JoDee on the ropes, he began dating. He eventually split from JoDee and had two more marriages, of a briefer duration. "He was without a doubt a restless soul," Ron says of him.

For the next few years he also began to address his

spiritual needs. Dealing with his father's and brother's deaths, his bout with alcoholism left him with nagging questions to which he needed answers.

A restless spirit, he tried a lot of things. "He always looked like he was uncomfortable with himself, or was trying to find something that wasn't there," says one woman who knew him then.

He'd traveled to the eastern United States to visit a school of enlightenment, and returned with an interest in organic gardening and meditation. "He was very intelligent, compassionate, spiritual, and very, very thoughtful," says Cheryl Tangen. "He was also very meditative and metaphysical." His meditation, at least in part, was due to something he told Cheryl about his life. "He once said that his life was like a chain and there was a link missing," she recalls. "I think he was always searching for that link. The most happy I ever saw him was when he was meditating or working in the garden. He loved flowers and yard work."

By the early 1990s, Larry had settled down a bit, and spending time with Cheryl Tangen seemed to be the rudder he needed to steady his life. Days spent working in the garden and meditating offered the peace he needed and relished.

Meanwhile, in his work, he became a charismatic man often seen on television in commercials, which made him a local celebrity. "He was so good in front of the camera," Cheryl says. "He was a natural, and the camera loved him."

Like Elisa, Larry had metamorphosed many times in his life. By 1995 the dapper ladies' man lawyer had gone through four wives. He'd gone from a high-

powered criminal defense attorney to being a highly
paid personal injury lawyer. And he'd gone from alcoholism to rehab and finally to a gardener who was
peacefully attentive to his flowers.

Elisa, though, presented him with something he also
enjoyed—having a good time. It was Elisa's specialty
and she loved it even more when someone else paid the
bill. But she also wanted to cherish the freedom she believed money brought her. She didn't care about meditation, or gardening, or anything pastoral and peaceful.
She was all rough edges and darkness, and that enticed
Larry as much as his peaceful pursuits.

When Elisa Barasch Redelsperger came tripping
into his life, Larry had settled down after his four previous marriages and had been dating and living with
Cheryl Tangen for seven years. "She was a master at
manipulation. She molded herself into whatever she
needed to get into someone's life," Cheryl says of
Elisa. "I think he hired her in July and he left me in August. She just made herself available to him 24/7."

The amount of energy and effort Elisa expended to
pry Larry from Cheryl can't be underestimated. He
and Cheryl were bound together as tightly as a married
couple. They spent a lot of time together, and Cheryl
was even involved in Larry's work, having written
some of his commercials with him. "I suggested let's
get him out of the suit and put him around town,"
Cheryl recalls. "It worked." She was also his meditation companion, his gardening pal, and one of his best
friends. "I still miss my buddy," she says of Larry.

No matter. Within a month of hiring Elisa, Larry
dropped his longtime companion and took up with the

leggy Brooksville, Florida, bombshell who was on the run from the law. It may not have been just for the sex either. Although her many paramours described her as an adequate lover, it was her gift of gab and her ability to ensconce herself in the open hole in someone's life that seemed the overwhelming factor in her knack of getting what she wanted.

"I was in awe of her," Cheryl said. "I couldn't believe he would fall for it. I'd ask Larry if he saw what she was doing to him, and he didn't see it. He thought she was a very vulnerable little girl."

Her manipulation knew no bounds. She began cutting and dying her hair like Cheryl's. Elisa was very dark, with dark hair, and Cheryl is a fair-haired blonde, but it didn't keep her from adopting a more exotic, Cheryl-like appearance for Larry. At the same time, she was adept at pushing Cheryl out of the picture. One day they happened to see each other in traffic while on the way to work. "I had the great misfortune of going down the same stretch of road to the office that Elisa took," Cheryl explains. "One day I see her at a stoplight, and the next thing I know Larry is calling me accusing me of stalking her."

Larry thought as much because when she got to work that day, Elisa immediately told him, apparently for no reason other than to manipulate him, that Cheryl was stalking her. When he confronted Cheryl, she laughed it off. "I said to him, you've known me seven years. I would never do anything like this." Larry shrugged. Maybe he believed her and maybe he didn't. What mattered was that Elisa stayed in his life.

Soon, Elisa found herself in almost total control.

She ran Larry's office, helped get him dressed, and arranged his meals. And it seemed that suited him just fine. He had always felt weighted down by his responsibilities and always wanted the freedom to explore life without those constraints. And Elisa, running the law firm, settled cases with a flair that others envied. Larry couldn't say enough about how aggressive and determined she was. She even managed to intimidate insurance company executives—people who often intimidated others.

But while he found his new girlfriend as "ruthless as he was," some of his friends found her to be something else. They couldn't quite put their finger on it. She was elusive and not easy to pin down about anything, especially concerning her past. She changed the subject when questioned, or gave vague often meaningless answers.

Tom Mitchell, a Reno lawyer, later told the *St. Petersburg Times*, "You could ask her where she went to high school, and pretty soon you'd be talking about skiing. Something wasn't right."

Ken Redelsperger had had a similar experience regarding the nonexistent furniture in her empty apartment. No one could figure out what it was about the woman that didn't add up.

Larry couldn't figure it out either.

When she first came to work with him, she said she had a master's degree in business. After a while, even though he'd broken up with Cheryl, he still confided in her. "I don't think [Elisa] told me the truth about her education," he said.

One day after they moved in together, Larry found

her stealing money from his wallet. He didn't leave her, nor kick her out. She had ingratiated herself too well for that, knew how to stay close to her host, even as she sucked him dry.

A few months later some of Larry's clients began to complain. More than $74,000 in client funds were missing from accounts. As it turned out, Larry's new office manager had used the client's money from a trust account to pay operating expenses and other obligations at his Las Vegas office. The bar reprimanded Larry in 1995 for the actions.

But he didn't fire Elisa or throw her out for that infraction. Instead, he decided to do what Ken Redelsperger had done. He married her.

"All I can say is, she must've been something in the sack," Bath says. "I knew Larry. He could have any woman he wanted. She had to have something for him to stay with her."

After all, Larry wasn't naive. He'd spent years dealing with the dark end of the criminal justice system. As partners, he and Ron had been very good at sniffing out con artists. "We had gotten taken by a story once or twice," Bath explains. "But we would often just look at each other while we were listening to a story, and we could tell a guy was trying to con us. So, for him to get hoodwinked by that woman, well, either he wanted to look the other way or she was a great, great con artist."

It may have been a bit of both. However, even as he got more involved with Elisa and got into trouble because of her, Larry did not lose his business sense completely. He decided to move the bulk of his firm from Nevada to Sacramento, where he was also admitted to practice law. He wanted a fresh start, and while he began to see what his new girlfriend and soon-to-be wife was really all about, he couldn't get rid of her. She filled many of his needs and he wanted her to stay, at least for a while longer as he explored the dark side of his psyche with her.

"She encouraged his drinking," Cheryl said. "He never drank in front of me. We never did that type of thing. But I think the fact is that she got him drunk because he was easier to control that way. I think he saw her as the ultimate thrill ride. There were no boundaries with her. She was an addiction, a drug. She was like a game on the edge, and Larry loved the edge."

By then Elisa was telling friends that not only was Larry drinking too much, but that he had begun to beat her. Newspaper accounts at the time of his death said that he physically abused and terrorized some of his previous wives, although prosecutor Tom Testa, who ultimately tried the case against Elisa McNabney's conspirator, Sarah Dutra, said he never found any evidence of abuse in Larry's background.

In fact there was some evidence, though not to the extent of wife-beating. It involved JoDee Bebout, Larry's second wife. Their fight took place long after their divorce, and came at the end of a frustrating day. Both JoDee and Larry found themselves yelling at each other when it got out of hand, leading to pushing and shoving. The case eventually became a misdemeanor. "I sided with my dad on that one," Tavia Williams later said. "Mom could get pretty upset herself."

JoDee said she never should have called the police on Larry that day, and knows how Elisa twisted the events to make Larry sound like an abuser. "Larry was almost passive in the way he handled the children," she says. "I don't think he would ever lay a hand on the kids, and he never laid a hand on me the entire time we were married. I can't see him hitting and beating women like Elisa said he did. At the same time, when I called the police, I did it because I wanted my children to know it wasn't all right to lay hands on me either."

Elisa's complaints that Larry had beaten her either right after they started dating or right after they got married, depending on which story is examined, flies in the face of logic, as does the story that Elisa felt she couldn't escape Larry, especially since she had her own car and controlled the law office's finances.

In addition, there is some anecdotal evidence that it was Larry who was beaten, not Elisa. Joe McNabney remembered a time, not too long before his father died, when he visited. He and Larry sat outside in the back sipping a beer and talking and Larry began to tease Elisa's dog, a small mixed-breed called "Munchie," also known as Morgan. Elisa responded by smacking Larry on the head repeatedly and screaming at him. Larry laughed, or tried to. Joe was flabbergasted. "I didn't know what to think," he says. "But I saw it happen."

But evidence of Larry being a chronic abuser is thin, and those who knew him say it was a fabrication. While everyone who knew Larry said you could get mad at him but couldn't stay mad, and that while he could be mean, vindictive, sarcastic, and a "smart ass," neither Ron Bath nor Larry's other friends ever saw him get physically violent with women.

Still, some say they remain convinced that Larry did strike Elisa. Her daughter, Haylei, and Sarah Dutra, have said as much. Did Elisa con them both into believing Larry struck her, or was it the truth? It is an issue that can never be resolved since both Elisa and Larry are now dead.

At any rate, there came a time when the ideal marriage of economic convenience for Elisa and the ideal marriage to a young trophy wife for Larry wasn't so ideal anymore.

After his death, Elisa tried to make it sound as if it began with the alleged beatings. But those close to the scene who knew both of them say the beginning of the end coincided with the hiring of a young secretary that many acquaintances also said was a better con artist than Elisa.

As Larry and Elisa became closer, they spent so much time together that it was impossible for Elisa to continue to do the work at the law firm for which she'd been hired. She later claimed that she had begun to play nursemaid to Larry, who was fighting off bouts of depression and suicidal thoughts of rage as his drinking and drug taking escalated. For that reason, she hired a secretary, and ganged up on by the two of them, Larry McNabney eventually lost his life to the dark side.

Cheryl Tangen doesn't find that hard to believe. "He was always talking about being seduced by the 'dark side,'" she says, "and so a couple of us who knew him real well would call him 'Captain Midnight.'"

It was the type of foreshadowing someone with Elisa's instinct for drama would have loved.

5

It's Hard to Handle This Fortune and Fame

After Laren was captured in Destin, Florida, the police who conducted her interview got an earful. She told them everything they wanted to know and many things they didn't. She volunteered that she had eventually told Larry, sometime during their relationship, that she was on the lam. She apparently never told him her real name, but confessed to him that she was on the run from Florida because of credit card fraud.

Not long after she began to date Larry, she also contacted her lawyer back in her hometown. She arranged to see Tom Hogan on a ski trip he took out West, told him she wanted to clean her past up because things were going so well for her and she'd finally gotten her life together. But when he came out, she'd changed her mind. Later, while in jail, she told Hogan that she hadn't gone to see him because Larry told her not to, and threatened to take Haylei away and turn her—Elisa—in to the police if she gave him any problems.

After she found herself in custody, Elisa—who by then had become Laren again—said Larry had begun hitting her just after she met him. "He started hitting me July 2, 1995," she told police. "I didn't want to make any waves because my daughter was in the house." She added that Larry had threatened to take her daughter away from her if she didn't straighten out. However, on July 2, 1995, Haylei wasn't living in Larry's house. According to Ken Redelsperger, Haylei was still living with him at the time. He hadn't yet shipped her to Elisa and Larry in California.

According to Laren, her life had become an endless nightmare in which Larry sat in his room drinking, watching pornography, snorting coke, and occasionally slapping her around. He didn't want to work and wouldn't make money. She said she took it upon herself to buy him a horse to get him involved in something, but even that was a challenge.

In a letter to Tom Hogan that Laren penned from jail just before she committed suicide, she didn't mention her daughter being present at the time of the first beating and gave a different date—exactly one year later—than she'd previously cited. She wrote that she immediately called a friend to tell her about the alleged beating, and later showed her bruises on her back and legs to verify the brutality Larry visited upon her.

"He always made the marks where they could be hidden," she explained.

In Laren's version of events, her life became unbearable as Larry began resembling a young Ozzy Osbourne, with his Neanderthal-like, drug-induced escapades. When he got tired of drinking, she said, the heavy drugs would kick in, and then things got really ugly. Larry would get verbally abusive, physically violent, and all but psychotic in his rants. But, according to Laren, she put her best foot forward and struggled valiantly to take care of her misguided husband. Getting him involved in quarter horses was one attempt, getting him into rehab was another, all while Larry hid his true nature from his friends and children. The night she confessed to Larry's murder, she told the police that only she got to see Larry's dark side, and it was full of powerful and potentially dangerous demons she could neither contain nor tame.

That Laren's description of her life with Larry would vary so much from a lifetime of his known activities is not incongruous with the way she described many situations in her life. "If she said the sun rises in the east, I'd check it to make sure," some of her closest friends said of her after they discovered that she wasn't who she said she was.

According to Laren's police interview, Larry began bringing prostitutes into their home, and so she shipped her daughter off to private school to get Haylei out of the caustic atmosphere in the home. Meanwhile, she stayed behind and struggled, nurturing the business and working at the job, securing Larry's income even as he seemed intent on spending it all on booze, drugs, loose women, quarter horses, and golfing.

Others tell a different tale. As early as December 1995, according to California sheriff's deputies who investigated Larry McNabney's murder, he had hired Dean Albright, a Reno CPA, because his office was under investigation by the Nevada State Bar. Elisa, in just a few short months, had embezzled money from his clients' trust fund as well as from his personal accounts.

According to the sheriff's report, Larry told Albright that he had a dating relationship with Elisa Redelsperger. According to Laren, in her subsequent confession in Florida, they were already married, and Larry had begun systematically beating her. Perhaps she considered herself married because she was apparently living with Larry at the time, but according to records, they had yet to tie the knot.

At any rate, Albright conducted an investigation and found that $74,543 had been lifted from the firm and its clients to maintain the couple's lavish lifestyle. Albright advised Larry to "get Elisa out of the office."

Larry did, firing Elisa and hiring another office manager.

About that time, on Christmas Eve, 1995, Larry showed up at the house of his former girlfriend, Cheryl Tangen, crying and upset. Why? It was Elisa, of course. He broke down and told Cheryl how Elisa had embezzled money from his business and personal accounts. He claimed he'd kicked Elisa out of the house they were sharing. He'd had enough.

He even had Cheryl drive by the house a few times with him to see if Elisa had left. "He was petrified of Elisa," she told investigators, and didn't want Elisa to know he was driving by to check up on her. Larry spent the following three days, including Christmas, with Cheryl, before he went back to his own home.

So, what happened next? According to Cheryl, Larry and Elisa were married in the first weeks of 1996. Happy New Year.

Although he married Elisa, he would, according to Cheryl, seek her friendship and advice regarding his wife at least one more time. In the fall of 1996 he came to stay with Cheryl for two more days. This time Larry told her he felt trapped in his relationship with Elisa and couldn't find a way to get out of it. According to investigators, he left Cheryl on an ominous note: If anything happened to him, he wrote, Elisa would be the one responsible.

Cheryl didn't know what to think.

On May 6, 1997, Larry went before the Nevada bar for Elisa's embezzlement and was reprimanded. But a week later, he fired his new office manager and reinstated his wife. It was typical of Elisa's method of operation. Those close to Larry were edged out in her favor. She controlled everything she could, either through coercion, intimidation, or removal. It was the last straw for Dean Albright. He told Larry he could no longer work as his accountant because Elisa was back in command.

But in the case of the misappropriated money, the other shoe still had to fall—a subsequent hearing before the Supreme Court of the State of Nevada. In *Re Discipline of Laurence W. McNabney*, No. 30465, Mar. 23, 1998, Larry accepted a conditional guilty plea, received a public reprimand, and paid the cost of the disciplinary proceedings. He also had to agree to two hours of legal ethics education. Additionally, the court said, "McNabney shall be the only signatory on his client trust account for the duration of his practice of law in Nevada." Then the document spelled out how

Elisa bilked his clients and used the funds for business expenses.

"It was all about his wife. Everyone involved in the case knew it," said one lawyer involved in the proceedings who requested anonymity. "Let me tell you. Everyone there knew the problem was Elisa. We tried to talk to him time and again. He wasn't the first guy to get in trouble because of his wife. But nothing we said to him seemed to matter."

In fact, the last stipulation—that Larry could be the only signatory on his client trust account—might be the real reason he closed up his Reno office and moved the bulk of his work to Sacramento. The whole thing had drained him, and he confessed to friends he was tiring of the law anyway. He was tired of the hassles and the hustles to make a buck, and told his friends he "wanted more."

Larry may have tried to shrug it off, but the reprimand was especially devastating to him. A man who was so worried about how a secretary typed a letter because it reflected on his reputation was not a man to take the news of a bar reprimand with ease. Larry had a conscience, not to mention an elevated standing in his community, which brought with it a certain comfortable lifestyle.

As had happened to him so many times before, he turned back to drinking to drown his sorrows and problems. His new wife had literally driven him to drink, although Elisa reported he had been taking heroin and other nefarious drugs, spending time with young nubile hookers and generally wasting away.

There was, as was usual with Elisa's lies, a kernel of truth to it. Larry was beginning to drink incessantly, and his friends saw it and blamed his wife. She blamed everyone else. He continued to drink. Finally, one day toward the end of his life, his behavior led to a police pursuit during which, according to his wife, he ran and hid and then jumped over his back fence to avoid being arrested.

The story is questionable for a variety of reasons, but primarily because Larry, as a criminal lawyer, knew well how to manipulate the system without resorting to hopping fences and running down the road while police looked for him. Still, his wife claimed that's what he did, and she reprimanded him for it. Those intricate details never made it into a police report.

"Larry, you need to get your shit together," she told him at the time, according to her videotaped confession in Florida. "He said, 'I'm not going to jail' . . . and our neighbor saw him because of reports of a prowler running around and they found him in the Albertsons parking lot and brought him back."

According to Elisa, Larry threatened to kill her in March 2000, checked in and out of rehab several times, and generally acted like a crazed lunatic. The picture she paints in her confession at times doesn't sound logical, although it does sound terrifying. She said Larry was doing eight-balls of cocaine, smoking and snorting crack, taking Xanex, smoking heroin to come down from the coke, and drinking so much wine that when Elisa walked into their home, it was literally littered with wine bottles.

At times like this, Elisa later told police, Larry was at

his worst: sarcastic, violent, and exceedingly temperamental. It was all she could do to get him into rehab.

However, once she got him there, and despite all of his problems, Elisa says she helped bust Larry out of rehab after he called her on her cell phone and urged her to visit. And though she went to elaborate lengths to describe the threat she felt Larry posed against her and even her daughter, whenever Haylei was home from school, Elisa still stayed with him. "Because every time I would say I want to leave him, he would say that he was going to kill me or kill Haylei," she told police.

Others say that at the time, to all appearances, Larry and Elisa looked like a fairly happy couple. As Elisa began to take over more of the daily work in his Sacramento office, Larry was free to pursue his budding hobby of owning and training quarter horses.

The horse show circuit fit Larry and Elisa like a velvet glove. He slid right into the gentle comradery, the easygoing nature of the people involved and the Jack Kerouac–like life on the road. For her part, Elisa had grown up around them in the rural confines of Florida and found horses easier to handle than people: They never made you steal Christmas presents, they weren't out to arrest you or do you harm, and if you treated them well, you could count on them to reciprocate. It had a soothing effect on her to be around horses, and she too liked being on the road, traveling and enjoying the good life without having to do any work. It is no coincidence that one of Ken Redelsperger's fondest memories of Elisa was of spending time with her and Haylei as the two girls rode horses on the beach.

Elisa's love of horses was one of the few pure things in her life. She liked them without thinking of ways to take advantage of them, although it wasn't above her to manipulate others so she could ride horses.

As Larry and Elisa got used to life on the road, they became close friends with Larry's trainer, Greg Whalen. The septuagenarian became a mentor to Larry, which former flame Cheryl Tangen said was a great relationship for Larry because he was always looking for a father figure after his own father died. Greg also became a confidant and a close friend to Elisa, with some people saying it looked as if Greg had a "little crush" on the younger woman.

Still, nothing seemed to be improper about the relationship between them, and it was good times all around for the McNabneys on the road. Larry was the life of the party and everybody knew him, and he made it a point to know everyone. He was the dapper dresser who would take the stage with as much aplomb as his favorite horse. He had a sense of humor and was down to earth. He bailed people out when they were in trouble, and he and Elisa became the "first couple" of the quarter horse circuit as well as the rising stars.

"So, with all that going on, how could Elisa's claims about Larry being this drug-addled psychotic be true?" Cheryl says. "He was never like that. Not when we were together. It's just another one of those lies she told."

"I thought Dad and her were at least enjoying themselves," his daughter Tavia says. "They pretty much did whatever they wanted."

Theirs was a life others could only dream about.

Glamorous travel to other cities, dining in restaurants, having maids take care of their every need in hotels across the country seemed to be Elisa's dream come true, but at the pinnacle of all this fun and frivolity, things went sour.

About a year before his death, Larry disappeared for several days on the road, only to show up sitting in the passenger side of his Mercedes with an unknown man driving him around. Friends in the neighborhood who saw the display shook their heads. The first time it happened, Elisa tried desperately to hide his behavior from his horse circuit friends. It wasn't the only time that Larry would disappear, though.

His friends worried about his drinking, and a few even mentioned it to Elisa, who in turn told them that everything was under control, or that she was getting him help at a rehab, or that Larry knew he had a problem and wanted to go to rehab, or that he had just busted out of a rehab, or any of a number of variations of those themes. While she seemed to try to appease his friends, they also say her stories often contradicted each other.

Meanwhile, his friends also say the fun and games continued and he was spending "buckets of money" on his new favorite pasttime, his quarter horses. It apparently wasn't money wasted, as he rang up thirty-three wins in fifty-two shows with his horse Justa Lotta Page.

He had entered the horse in what was essentially an equine beauty show, and he was as much on display as his horse. He'd lead his unsaddled stallion into the ring for judging, sporting one of his huge, engaging grins, and then he would walk with the horse slowly around the ring. The crowds invariably fell in love with both the owner and the horse.

But while this was all going on in front of the crowds in the short months prior to his death, backstage, Larry's friends began to distance themselves from Elisa, who was not endearing herself to anyone, except perhaps to a few drug dealers and a new best buddy. Some say her new companion looked a lot like the actress Jennifer Aniston, and the two of them were seen backstage smoking marijuana, occasionally grinning uncontrollably after ingesting a few cans of nitrous oxide in the form of "whippets," and sometimes popping stray pills.

By the fall of 2000, Larry and Elisa seemed to be not only on a downward spiral, but heading for a collision course. Elisa was increasingly late getting to the office, and got into fights with Larry over the mess the business had become. Money was beginning to get tight, even though their lavish spending continued freely. Larry, having hired Elisa as his secretary, wanted her to do something about it. Since becoming his wife, however, Elisa had decided that Larry needed to take care of the business while she enjoyed the good life. Neither of them wanted to compromise on what they felt the other was responsible for, and meanwhile they both continued to party hard.

It was at about this time that Elisa lost a little of the control she was well known for. She had successfully squeezed both of Larry's daughters out of his life, minimized his son Joe's involvement and that of all of Larry's ex-wives and girlfriends. But maintaining such tight control was getting to her. The cracks began to show in her thin veneer of civility.

It manifested itself in different ways. For one, she began to routinely screen all the mail that came into Larry's office. And she got into loud fights with her own daughter. Those closest to her saw the effects of her prolonged use of not only marijuana, but alcohol, diet pills, and even cocaine. She came into the office less than her professional best on a few occasions and publicly complained about Larry spending too much money and forcing her to work to pay his bills. Others overheard her on the telephone lying to her daughter about the events in her life, her whereabouts as well as Larry's. They also heard her lying to Larry's son and daughters, and to Larry as well.

Both Larry and Elisa were burned out for different reasons. Larry wanted Elisa to pick up the slack, and she wanted him to do more. But the effect was the same. Neither one of them could come to terms with what needed to be done to run the company more efficiently and with greater profits. Still, Larry didn't seem to care, and had proven that by putting Elisa in charge. It was quite a climb for a girl who'd begun life in tiny Brooksville, Florida. But she wasn't happy about it.

Instead, she seemed put out and irate. Larry was having the fun and she was working. Her ruthlessness had been successful when she first came on board, squeezing money out of insurance companies, but she ultimately began running the business into the ground. Larry didn't have the energy to deal with it and wasn't bringing in the clients as he once had. He knew he had to get rid of Elisa, but he couldn't do that either. All he wanted to do was to spend his time golfing, enjoy his friends and family, and have fun with the horses. That's when he got drunk on the golf course downing vodka lemonades, ended up running someone off the road on Highway 99 near Elk Grove, and Elisa painted the crazed, lunatic scenario of Larry hopping over fences and running around the neighborhood until he was found at a nearby local grocery store.

Whatever actually happened that night, Elisa began complaining about Larry in public and the marriage began to tank. Both Larry and Elisa seemed desperately unhappy, despondent, and unable to do anything about the mess they were in.

The question many of Larry's friends and family wanted answered was: Why did it happen then? What was the black magic that turned everything around and sent the couple down into their colliding spiral?

The catalyst was Sarah Dutra, and with her around at the beginning of the new millennium, things were about to get much worse.

6

Sarah Smiles

Sarah Dutra entered Larry's and Elisa's lives in as haphazard a fashion as Elisa had entered Larry's. She needed a job. She was in college, wanted some extra spending money, and found an ad Elisa had placed in the newspaper for a legal secretary.

From the beginning, in the late spring of 2000 when Sarah came to work for Larry, she and Elisa became close friends. Both were tall, good-looking women who complemented each other when seen in public. Sarah was in her twenties with long blondish hair. They listened to each other's gripes and complaints, shared an intense love of shopping and the finer things in life. Both women were also somewhat messy in their personal habits, leaving their work stations unkempt and their beds unmade. They were, in many ways, the essence of J. D. Salinger's "Secret Slob." They always looked good, but trashed everything around them to get that way.

Sarah shared Elisa's love for pop culture. If she didn't see her life as a movie, then she certainly saw herself as being a celebrity. Her high school yearbook has a personal page in it with her kitschy philosophy of life highlighted. "Always Lead. Never Follow." The saying was cut out from a magazine ad she admired. So was a picture of Calvin Klein perfume, a Nike logo, a Levi's jeans logo for women, and similar icons. "I don't need astrology hotlines. I'd rather find the answers myself, shopping" was another saying of hers, made from sentences clipped out of a couple of magazines.

The attractive young woman had grown up in an upper-middle-class environment. She went to high school in Vacaville, a town between San Francisco and Sacramento, where she was an above-average student. She was also on the drill team, student council, and trained to throw the discus. She graduated in the top ten percent of her class in 1998, and her principal, Wayne Mills, told a local reporter, "She was an outstanding student and was very involved in the school life here. She was the senior class president."

Sarah Dutra. Senior class '98. Class President. Drill team member. Best friend. Murderer.

In the year or so before she met Elisa, while an art student at California State University, Sarah sported her own Web page, which proudly invited everyone to take a look at a variety of her views on the more pressing issues of our time. Among them, she talked about things she looked for in guys:

1. Great hands
2. A good sense of humor

3. A desire to Go, Go, Go all the time!
4. Great lips

Her website also told everyone, "I am an art student, with high hopes of graduating this spring, and will continue on to graduate school ASAP!!! I know this must sound crazy, but I love school and never want to stop . . . it sure beats being a grown up!!!" She also told everyone her her favorite places on earth were San Francisco; Florence, Italy; and Sacramento, California. She happily offered dining advice to those interested in visiting her favorite cities, citing the Grande Café in San Francisco, Una Bella Serra in Florence, and the China Dragon in Sacramento as excellent places to enjoy a night out.

Those who knew Sarah in college genuinely liked her, finding her outgoing and fun-loving. She was very interested in surrealistic paintings and developed a fan base of close friends who enjoyed her efforts.

Few who knew her could fathom a darker side of her life. One exception was a Vacaville police officer, for whom Sarah Dutra used to work as a babysitter. "He said she was the most self-centered, narcissistic bitch he'd ever met," says one of the officers who ultimately investigated Larry's death.

Sarah had her troubles too. Her father had a checkered past with the law, which included embezzlement of church funds, according to prosecutor Tom Testa, but she didn't seem to have a chip on her shoulder about it. Other than the comment about narcissism, the worst anyone else could offer about Sarah was that she appeared to be spoiled. Some say she was rude to her parents in public on occasion, but most who met her described her as a friendly young woman who had a cheery temperament and was very attractive—not unlike her soon-to-be boss, Elisa McNabney.

"You wanna know who Sarah Dutra was, take a look at Elisa McNabney," says Deborah Scheffel, a police officer who investigated the McNabney murder.

Sarah's friend Mike Sullivan couldn't have disagreed more. He told a reporter, "When you think about Sarah, I think of a great student . . . she was an absolutely remarkable young lady. I'm frankly floored. You know how sometimes you think something's not happening? This is it. You can't imagine this happening, not even in your wildest dreams."

Her high school music director, John Phillips, said the same thing, and so did another childhood friend, Elie Debevec, who told local reporters that Sarah Dutra was always a cut above most other people: "She's always been great; a great friend, a great person. She never had a mean bone in her body. . . . She's always been the leader type. She's always enjoyed people, meeting everyone, [being] creative." Debevec knew Sarah in elementary school and served on the student council with her in high school. "The last two years of school, we planned all the floats and the prom," Debevec recalls. "We planned the decorations and getting everything organized, and the winter ball. She was an awesome friend to me. When I had a hard time in high school, she was there. She was dedicated and honest."

Later, upon her arrest, Sarah told police that she "never had an enemy in my life; never had anyone who hated me. Never felt threatened before by another person—ever." As for what type of person she was, Sarah told police she "felt like I didn't fit in. I started liking myself more in high school. I was neither a leader nor a follower. I was nice to everyone. I liked to stay to myself."

Her life after high school hardly seems to be that of an honest person—especially after she met and began working for Larry and Elisa McNabney. Those around her during that time said Sarah was as adept at lying and manipulating as Elisa, and she did it "almost more" convincingly.

In the office environment where she worked, others noticed that Elisa and Sarah looked to be attached at the hip. Joe McNabney didn't like it and said as much. "I only met her two or three times," he says. "She was weird. She talked about marijuana constantly." The secret of life was pot, according to Sarah. It made you smarter and you could "think beyond other realms." Joe didn't fathom nor like the philosophy of marijuana according to Sarah Dutra. "She was like a weird hippie chick, but worse," he said. "Not that there's anything wrong with being a hippie."

Whatever it was Joe didn't like about Sarah—her preaching the gospel according to cannabis sativa, or her forward nature, or her seeming infatuation with Elisa—Larry liked her even less, and told several of his friends that Sarah was horning her way into his life and he wanted it to stop.

The question was, why didn't he fire her? The answer was Elisa. When people had seen her upset in the past, they'd used descriptive terms like "out of control" or a raging "volcano of emotion" to describe the displays they'd witnessed. It was no great stretch to see that Larry wanted to avoid that confrontation and all its ramifications.

All Larry wanted was to relax and enjoy the golf course and his horses. But Sarah and Elisa weren't going to even let him do that. The situation became unbearable for him, and Larry became increasingly lonely, isolated, and bitter. There was a good reason for this. Early in their relationship, Elisa had diverted any and all attention and affection from Larry that was given by anyone she thought was too close to him, or anyone she determined who could be a rival for his affections. Elisa engineered the isolation that would contribute to his spiraling infatuation with alcohol that would indirectly lead to his death.

His son Joe, with whom Larry longed to have a good relationship, appeared to be a notable exception to the control Elisa had over Larry's involvement with other people. Elisa permitted this, according to Joe's mother, Jodee, because Elisa had it in the back of her mind to seduce Joe if she got the chance.

Otherwise, she often played the same game with Joe that she played with everyone else. Elisa would refuse to take his call, or wouldn't return the call, or wouldn't pass along vital information to Larry about his only son. John Kelly, coauthor of the book *Warning Signs*, about avoiding problems with children, is fond of saying that boys need fathers. But Elisa, if she was aware of the philosophy, couldn't have cared less. Boys may need fathers, but Elisa needed control. So sometimes she would tell Joe that Larry wasn't available to talk to him when in fact Larry was around.

For Tavia Williams it was even worse. Her dad had been by her side when she got married, but Elisa had been so successful in keeping her out of Larry's life that Tavia never even met Haylei, and she didn't see Elisa more than a handful of times in six years.

"She was sweet as butter to me the first time we met," Tavia says of Elisa. Then after that, "I couldn't get ahold of my dad. He was never around. On Father's Day in 1996, I tried to get a present to him."

But she was unable to do it. Elisa told Larry that the young woman was stalking her.

Meanwhile, Sarah got a car, in Elisa's name—which caused problems with Haylei, who became jealous of her mother's closeness with her new friend. Taking Sarah under her wing, Elisa taught her how to spend clients' money while putting them off and how to squeeze as much money as legally or illegally possible from insurance companies. Sarah happily engaged in the subterfuge, eventually graduating into Elisa's class by bragging to others that she'd even managed to con Elisa.

Elisa, for her part, saw Sarah as a soulmate. The relationship even allegedly took on a sexual flavor, with Larry telling a friend of his that he caught Sarah "fucking" his wife. Others who knew them said it couldn't have been more than experimentation, if in fact they actually ever did sleep together. Ginger Miller, a secretary in the McNabney office, said the two women were too homophobic and liked men too much to be serious lovers. Still, Ginger and others say the two women were as close as "husband and wife" after Sarah had been working at the firm a little more than two months.

Those who saw them said Sarah definitely "wore the pants" in the relationship, controlling and influencing Elisa far more effectively than Larry could.

It now appeared that Sarah dominated Elisa, and Larry was cut out. "I think Sarah wanted Elisa to herself," says a close friend. Larry's inability to deal with Elisa had given the keys to his kingdom to her, and eventually to Sarah, and they both proved to have the hearts of pirates.

"I cannot put into words how I feel about Sarah," Tavia says. "If Elisa hadn't met Sarah, my dad would be alive today."

"I really think Sarah was the biggest part of the murder," Larry's son Joe adds. "I saw Dad and Elisa together before Sarah came around. They laughed together and had fun. I believe Elisa really loved my dad. There's no way you could say they didn't love each other."

Successfully pushing Larry away from Elisa may have been Sarah's goal, but Sarah and Elisa still wanted Larry as a meal ticket, and that had became problematic. Larry had been reprimanded once by the bar, and he had no intention of going through that pain again. He'd already moved to Sacramento to avoid problems in Nevada, and probably should have notified the state about his previous problems. But the California state bar noted after his death that he had no problems there.

In the end, perhaps Larry simply couldn't turn over the keys to the kingdom to the extent that Elisa or Sarah wanted. His reputation couldn't afford it, nor could his pocketbook. He could be content hanging out on the back nine of his favorite golf course, or hitting the road with his favorite quarter horse, but only if he had a source of income—and more important, only if his reputation was intact. His wife was supposed to take care of that, but she had needed a secretary. The secretary was supposed to take care of it, but she needed Elisa. Larry had to fight back just for survival's sake, and that led to some loud arguments between him and Elisa. She would later characterize his behavior as he fought against her control as "evil."

Elisa was running the firm, but wanted to spend time with Sarah. Larry wanted his wife and his secretary to do their work. They just wanted his money, and became convinced they could do without him. It was a disaster waiting to happen.

To the outside observer, it would have seemed an odd triangle. Sarah and Larry never got along. Friends and acquaintances say Sarah actually avoided Larry because he would often get upset with her. It is possible that he didn't know himself how often Elisa and Sarah were together, but Larry made it clear on many occasions that he didn't like her around. And despite his concern about his wife's histrionics, he finally screwed up his courage and indignations enough to more than once urge Elisa to fire Sarah: But it never happened. Instead, the women grew even closer. They very much saw their situation as "you and me against the world," and when Sarah landed a coveted exchange student posting in Italy, Elisa went so far as to pay for several of her flights home to California so she could visit Elisa and, if she got the time, her parents. Once, according to Tom Testa, Elisa went so far as to pay for trips home on back-to-back weekends from Italy. The cost was no problem. Elisa controlled the cash flow into Larry's office. She had no trouble cooking the books to get what she wanted, even if cost Larry or his clients.

It drove Larry crazy. Not only wouldn't Elisa fire the lazy secretary, but after Sarah took off for Italy, Larry still had to see her because Elisa kept bringing her back.

Italy was a comfort for Sarah, but a nightmare for her landlady. According to Testa, Sarah was selling marijuana from the room she rented in Florence, and ripping off the elderly landlady who needed the money she was supposed to get from Sarah just to survive. Sarah apparently didn't care and, while on this trip— with frequent return visits paid for by Elisa—she bragged to college friends she was even ripping off her best friend.

When she got back from Italy, Daniel Nordas, who had two art classes with Sarah before she traveled abroad, told the college newspaper: "Before she went to Italy, I talked to her about the trip and her drawings. When she came back, I heard about how great the trip was, how great living in Florence was."

When Sarah got back from Italy, she and Elisa spent almost all their waking hours together. Elisa complained bitterly about Larry, saying he was unstable and often drunk. Her behavior may have driven him to it, but in her mind it was entirely his fault, and she was angry about it. Many of the couple's friends backed away as Elisa displayed her venomous anger by ranting and raving, but Sarah didn't mind. She drew closer to Elisa, so close that in the summer of 2001, Elisa leased an apartment for Sarah and her daughter Haylei near Larry's business and home. This did little to mollify the feelings of isolation Haylei was beginning to feel, since Sarah demanded more and more of her mother's time.

Later testimony showed that after Sarah and Elisa murdered Larry, all three women would sleep in the same bed in the McNabney house, while Larry's body was stuffed in the garage refrigerator, but Haylei was no more comfortable around Sarah than she was around Larry. Joe McNabney saw it and felt sorry for Haylei. "I hope she has it better now," he says, "because she didn't have it so good when she was with her mother."

Meanwhile, Joe's mother, JoDee, heard her son talking about Haylei and Elisa and became increasingly concerned for Joe. "I told him never be alone with either of those two," she says. Ironically, Larry—who would be killed when alone with his wife and Sarah—told his son the same thing.

For Haylei, life had become a bitter pill. It hadn't been good growing up on the lam with her fugitive mother, but her heartwrenching postcard to her brother Cole in Florida—found by Ken Redelsperger—in which she dreamed of a normal life, was just the tip of the iceberg of her pain. She didn't get along well with her mother at times, nor with Sarah, and most especially not with Larry.

He called her a spoiled brat on several occasions, which didn't endear him to her. He told Elisa her daughter was out of control and that Haylei was a whiner and "all about herself." Elisa's only response was to ship Haylei away to boarding school. In some ways, Haylei had become a roadblock for her mother, and it was convenient for Elisa to blame all of the mother-daughter problems on Larry, whose open hostility to the young lady was easily manipulated by Elisa's masterfully deceptive nature.

"Haylei never had it easy," Joe says.

JoDee adds, "I think in some ways she raised her mother more than Elisa raised her."

Haylei recounted how, as a child, she helped her mother on many occasions, including making sure Elisa got up in the morning to go work. Haylei also became concerned with her mother's nutrition and tried to get her to eat right. After her mom died, Haylei said she didn't want to complain about those efforts. According to her, Elisa would do anything to help her out in times of need. She vividly recalled an event, for instance, that touched her, a time when her mother stayed up all night making a costume for Haylei that was needed at school. "I loved her very much and I knew what she was," Haylei later said. There is little doubt that the two cared deeply for each other, and there is also little doubt that Sarah encroached on the relationship.

Ultimately, Elisa would take Haylei on the run with her when she fled California after killing her husband, but before that, Sarah stole a lot of time away from mother and daughter. Part of it was because Elisa didn't want Haylei to witness some of the more unsavory things she did. Smoking dope and taking drugs while plotting murder wasn't the kind of wholesome mother-daughter activity Elisa had in mind with Haylei. She also might have kept her daughter at arm's length, to maintain some parental control.

Sarah's demanding nature also made it next to impossible for anyone else to be involved with Elisa beyond a cursory level. Although Larry, Haylei, Tavia, Cristin, and Joe didn't exactly see things eye-to-eye and sometimes fought among each other, they had a lot in common when it came to Elisa. They were all extremely dissatisfied with the relationship she had with Sarah. Elisa had been an effective roadblock in keeping people out of Larry's life, and Sarah proved the old adage that what's good for the goose is good for the gander by doing the same to Elisa.

Sarah's control could manifest itself in cruelty with Haylei. She and Sarah were sharing an apartment together, but whenever Sarah and Elisa wanted to be together without Haylei around, they told her that Sarah was going off to visit a "secret boyfriend," according to Ginger Miller, a woman Elisa and Sarah both hired after Larry's death to be their secretary.

Ginger said that once Sarah left the apartment, Elisa, who was at her own home, would take off on a previously arranged rendezvous with Sarah, leaving Haylei alone in the apartment while the two best friends enjoyed a night of mayhem and debauchery. The two women apparently often enjoyed fooling Haylei with this or a similar story.

As the relationship progressed between the two women, those who did not share in their special friendship began to express fear at being around them, especially after Larry disappeared, before his body was

found. Ginger, whose first day on the job in the Mc-
Nabney law firm working for Sarah and Elisa was the
same day that Larry was killed, expressed discomfort
being around them, as did Joe McNabney, who was invited to a party at his dad's house by Sarah when Larry
was missing. Joe didn't know it at the time, but he was
being invited to the house where his father had died.

Shortly before Christmas of 2001, Sarah called and
asked him to come by and party with her and Elisa. For
reasons he says he doesn't even fully understand to this
day, he did not feel comfortable with the invitation, and
remembering his mother's admonition about spending
time alone with Elisa, he turned down the request.

At about the same time, Ginger Miller received an
invitation to a nonexistent barbecue party that she
quickly turned down. In both cases it was Sarah who
extended the invitation, and she was the woman people
say was the more fearful of the two.

By the time Sarah and Elisa decided to kill Larry,
everyone who knew the women said Sarah was the one
firmly in control, giving orders to Elisa, setting up their
social calendar, running the business, and eventually
manipulating the events that led to Larry's death.

Joe, JoDee, Tavia, Cheryl, and everyone else who
knew Larry say Sarah had a huge, negative impact on
everyone around her. Her boldness and her own fear-
lessness were on display on the day before Larry's
death. Sitting at a dinner table with Greg Whalen, his
daughter, and Elisa, when Larry came down and saw
her having dinner with his closest friends and family,
she just said "Fuck you" when he questioned her presence at the table. It was the same bravado with which

she assisted in the plan to kill him. Sarah had become a cold, manipulating murderer whose metamorphosis came after answering a simple help wanted ad.

Elisa had found the raw material in the young Sarah to create a Frankenstein she could never control.

7

Don't Talk About It

By August 2001, long before Elisa and Sarah murdered Larry, things were so crazy in the McNabney law offices that little if any work was getting done. Larry was always golfing or spending time with the horses, and Elisa was either with him or with Sarah. Meanwhile, Larry was upset that Sarah, who was supposed to be doing the clerical work, was pulling down a paycheck but putting in fewer and fewer hours at the office and more and more hours out and about with Elisa.

He faced the unenviable task of hiring yet another secretary to do the work of the secretary who was hanging out with his wife—his first secretary.

Haylei, who sometimes worked in the office when she was around, was back East in school as September began, far from the haphazard and chaotic life in the law firm. Consequently, with so few people actually working, there was little income at the firm. Elisa realized that things had to change if she wanted to maintain her lifestyle. Someone had to file the cases, mail out the bills, cash the checks, and do the various little chores needed to keep Larry on the golf course and Sarah and herself in their Jaguars, Mercedes, Saabs, and fine clothes. Someone needed to do the work.

That's when Elisa decided, against Larry's will, to hire another secretary. Once again she placed an ad in the *Sacramento Bee*. An former exotic dancer, Ginger Miller, a beautiful young woman in her mid-twenties, answered the ad. "She's a character straight out of film noir," says prosecutor Tom Testa. "She has a real Marilyn Monroe look about her."

Tavia was ultimately one of the happiest to see Ginger hired. "I saw her in court," she says, "and she wasn't the type of woman my father would typically hire. But I am so thankful she did what we couldn't do. Without Ginger there may have never been a case against Elisa or Sarah."

"They were looking for a secretary, will train, so you didn't need any legal experience," Ginger said of the random event that would change her life. Answering the ad, she came to the law firm and was interviewed by Sarah Dutra. Ginger remembered the event clearly. "I think it was her first interview ever because she obviously didn't know what she was doing. They called me back like three or four days later and said they wanted to hire me and that Larry would call me back that day because he wanted to talk to me."

This was the first week of September 2001. She never did talk to Larry, but showed up at work for the first time on September 10. A few days before, Elisa had made plans to get rid of her daughter, at least temporarily. Haylei was just sixteen years old, but her mother decided once again to send her away to school—this time all the way across the country to a Maine horseback-riding school. Her mother told her it wasn't just for an education, but to protect her from Larry, who was jealous and constantly drunk.

"There were always problems between Larry and I," Haylei later testified, referring to sentiments Larry expressed about her being spoiled.

But according to Joe, there were also growing problems between Haylei and her mother, and it had to do with Sarah Dutra. Joe said he heard Elisa say, "I can't wait until she's gone," referring to Haylei. "I hate the little bitch."

It was tough for Joe because he had established a relationship with Haylei and genuinely felt bad for her. She'd introduced Joe as her big brother, for instance, whenever they met people, and she seemed to crave affection and attention from him. Joe didn't know about her brother Cole, but he does remember Haylei felt she had a brother in him.

"Where's my dad?" he would ask when he called and Haylei answered the phone.

"Don't you mean our dad?" she would respond, and Joe would humor her because he saw in her a young girl growing up without a family, with few friends, and with a manipulative mother who seemed distant at best. He believes Haylei was looking for a father figure in her life. When she ran off to raves in San Francisco, she'd later tell him about her latest male conquests. "I really felt sorry for her," he says.

Haylei's testimony in Sarah Dutra's trial would outline horrible living conditions, but it is hard to figure out what was real and what was fiction, mainly because Elisa had been very good at deceiving her own daughter. "Who knows what she told Haylei?" one of the investigators later said. "It's doubtful Elisa even remembered the lies she told from one day to the next."

Whatever Haylei was told, she evidently heard some strong disagreements between her mother and Larry, and she later said as much. This was in stark contrast to what Joe McNabney saw. He testified that Larry and Elisa got along very well, and he was convinced there was real affection between the two. In conversations, he recalls, Elisa was exceptionally intelligent, often spoke of the most minute intricacies of the law, and went toe-to-toe with Larry on any subject of his choosing. To Joe, the pair always seemed to get along fine.

The only exception he remembered was when he saw Elisa smack his father on the head while arguing about a dog. The event was memorable and notable to Joe because he thought it was out of character. "I wanted to say, you know, stop hitting my Dad," he says. "But Dad was laughing and I didn't know how to take it."

It was a side of Elisa's personality that she allowed few to see. Joe didn't like it, and later questioned his father about it. Larry shrugged it off. He also shrugged off the other major character flaw that Elisa displayed: her ability to spin the truth better than a spokesman for a presidential candidate.

Joe noticed her lies, and noted that men seemed to let her get away with it because of her charm and her looks, although he never found her particularly attractive. When he questioned Larry about his wife, her temper, and the way she spun the truth, Larry only shrugged that off too. Finally, settling for a nonsensical non sequitur, Larry told his son that Elisa was on medication for compulsive lying.

"I knew she was faulty," Joe later testified at the trial, voicing what may have been the single biggest understatement in the entire fiasco.

Faulty, she may have been, but in the summer of 2001, Elisa was definitely in charge of everything, except perhaps Sarah. She ran the law firm, ran Larry, ran her daughter, and any clients, vendors, lawyers, horse trainers, and stray animals that crossed her path.

She did it with flare, but she rarely did it early. On a typical workday Elisa would get up late, unless her daughter or someone else got her up on time. She'd have a light breakfast, especially if she was gobbling diet pills, then would shower and, hopefully, get into the office before noon. Once she arrived, she would take over like Captain Kirk at center stage, screening calls, directing traffic, dodging clients, and hustling in the money. She was particularly mindful of any calls from clients demanding money, or any calls regarding unhappy clients.

Masterful at evading people she wished to avoid, she would occasionally answer the phone and deny who she was, or say she was someone else. More than one person witnessed her telling someone on the telephone that Elisa wasn't there. Once the mail came, Elisa, by her own decree, was the only person allowed to touch it. After a while the only work that got done was her close inspection of the mail—usually just to see if there was a check she could deposit and spend.

Meanwhile, Sarah would spend the morning doing schoolwork in the office, or more often than not playing on the phone with a stray boy she caught in her web. By lunchtime, with all the little petty things like work out of the way, she and Elisa would take an extended lunch break. If Haylei was in town, she would be pressed into service to handle bookkeeping, phones, run errands, or do whatever work her mother asked her to do.

After Larry died, the routine changed little. Ginger Miller, the new girl on the block, picked up the pace and did most of the actual work in the office, while Sarah and Elisa did nothing more than what they wanted to do at the time.

"They were great at getting out of work," Ginger said. "They were so busy having a good time that they looked at work like some kind of nuisance."

Haylei was expected to work also, and if she wasn't around, then she and her mother kept in touch by phone. Ginger remembered these conversations as classic examples of the dynamic at work between Elisa and her daughter.

"Tell that bitch to get on the phone," Haylei would scream at her mother, using Ginger as an intermediary. Elisa would avoid speaking to her daughter, not only putting Ginger in the middle, but assuring escalating tension between the two. "Sometimes you'd think they liked to fight, you know," Ginger says. To her, the whole situation got to be ludicrous.

The rest of the workday, after arriving late and taking a long lunch, invariably ended with Elisa leaving early, usually with Sarah. From work, they might go shopping or look at new cars, or drive around and hit the pipe, smoking "killer weed" while driving around the countryside.

To avoid the side effects of consuming large amounts of marijuana, the two women also ingested diet pills to keep them reasonably coherent and active. The pills became such a big part of their lives that after Larry died, Ginger noted that Elisa had dropped several dress sizes and more than twenty pounds. During the few short months Ginger worked for the McNabney firm, Sarah's weight loss was even more dramatic.

When Elisa actually stayed in for an afternoon of work instead of hitting the town, she was seen screening more telephone calls, and avoiding contact with anyone except those who gave her money. By the end of the business day she was ready for an aperitif and a trip to one of Sarah's favorite restaurants, a deeply religious experience for Sarah, if her website can be believed. After dinner it was another hit off the pipe and more diet pills. Sometimes they took so many diet pills they skipped the evening meal all together. Then, according to Sarah, they might rent or see a movie, and if the mood struck them, they might drop some "X," have a few drinks and really get cranking.

This was the lifestyle the two women were leading as September 2001 approached. Larry, when he wanted to be around, frequently found himself at odds with his wife and secretary. The two women spent so much time together that it's likely any married man would have gotten cranky, even if he were invited along—which Larry wasn't. While Sarah was overseas, at least Larry saw his wife during the week if he wanted, but once Sarah returned, he couldn't get a moment with Elisa without it inevitably leading to a nasty fight with her or sometimes Sarah.

The only place Larry could overrule his wife about Sarah's presence was on the road with the quarter horses. That remained his domain, and consequently Sarah kept her distance. But the struggles between Larry and Elisa about Sarah's continued presence in their life was becoming impossible to overcome.

What Larry didn't know was that by the summer of that year, the two women had decided they just didn't want him around. Elisa had begun to joke about killing him, and she even told some of her acquaintances on the horse circuit that she'd spiked his drinks with Vicodin so she could get some time away from him. "I should just kill him," she said on more than one occasion. More than a few of these horse circuit friends who heard her say this thought she was making a joke, albeit a poor one. They backed away from her.

Sarah heard it and said, "Don't talk about it. Do it."

At first Elisa couldn't put her intentions into action. She wasn't at all comfortable with physically harming anyone, even though Sarah continued to tell her how extremely evil Larry was. To Elisa, he still had his good points, and she still felt some affection for him— a feeling she never could completely dismiss, and one that ultimately rubbed her raw with whatever guilt she was able to muster. She could take money from people to survive, she could take money from people to thrive, and she could take money from people just for the hell of it. Her motto was: Why work for it when you could steal it? But taking someone's life was an escalation of her career as a criminal she had no taste for—or so she thought.

What she wanted was the good, easy life of partying, ingesting chemicals, and avoiding all responsibility. She ultimately turned the responsibility for killing Larry over to Sarah after she became convinced that her single biggest roadblock to the happiness she wanted was Larry—the man who in fact made her entire lifestyle possible.

The lack of logic in that argument didn't bother Elisa. By midsummer she wasn't thinking very far down the road. She had always placed a high value on instant gratification, and by the end of August it was all she was thinking about, to the detriment of her own self-interest.

This change, brought upon her by Sarah, manifested itself in a shortness of temper at times and a lack of empathy for other people. And as she lost weight, and her mean streak grew, she became even more obsessed with shopping. She bought entire new wardrobes, and so did Sarah. On one occasion, a clerk at a local store said she watched as Elisa tried on thirty or forty different outfits. "She wasn't satisfied with anything and she wouldn't even look at it unless it was the most expensive thing we had," the clerk says. "You could tell she just looked down her nose at anything off the rack."

By the time Elisa was arrested for Larry's murder and was sitting in a South Florida jail cell, telling her turgid tale of woe, most of the pretentious nature she showed clerks, secretaries, and even some friends was gone. Stripped of the money, the clothes, and the other trappings of power, she said she thought of herself as the ugly, empty soul, the person others had seen.

Did she mean it? It's hard to say. Even in her confession, Elisa blatantly lied about the facts surrounding Larry's death. She lied so easily and so frequently in her confession that afterward few could piece together what was real and what was fantasy. Making it even more difficult to tell was the simple fact that Larry and Elisa were both dead and had been the only witnesses to certain key events.

Central to the prosecution's case was the belief that Sarah had an integral part in killing Larry, and with Larry dead, and after Elisa killed herself, it was hard to prove that Sarah was the catalyst to the fatal final act of Larry's life.

According to Elisa, things had been going badly even before Sarah Dutra came on the scene.

In October 1999, Elisa and Larry visited Kentucky for a horse show and also visited Michigan, Oregon, and several other states as they lived the high life on the road. "The whole time that we're on the road, we aren't making any money, but we're also not generating any clients," she explained. That worried her because with Larry's ability to run through money, combined with her own insatiable appetite for cash, she could see the handwriting on the wall. For a while, as the year 2000 rolled around, she began flipping assets back and forth from the company's general fund and trust funds to pay the steep bills they were incurring.

But she said Larry got mad at her for doing that, so mad that sometimes she would wake up and Larry "would be choking me." Elisa blamed his erratic and dangerous behavior on the drugs that she claimed he was ingesting. It was the drugs, she said, that were taking a toll on their marriage and his business. She believed that until Sarah came around, the firm was headed into the toilet. Elisa's overriding mantra was that it was all Larry's fault and that Sarah was the salvation. Sarah became her good friend who dispensed sage advice during the crisis and helped put the McNabney law firm back on solid ground.

It couldn't have happened at a better time, because in March 2000, Elisa claimed that Larry tried to shoot her, succeeding instead in shooting holes in the floor of the house. After that, still blaming events on Larry's drug use, she got him into rehab. A short time later, she claimed she broke him out of one rehab and got him into another one. And then after getting out of the rehab, she claimed that Larry beat her so badly he broke several bones in her face. Witnesses later refuted that, saying she had fallen during an accident and it was Larry who took care of her after she went to the doctor.

After the supposed gun incident, Elisa said she got Sarah and one of her occasional boyfriends to come to her house and empty the clip in Larry's handgun. Then she hid the gun in his office and put the bullets elsewhere. She was only trying to protect Larry, she said, because he was a "convicted domestic batterer or something." Later, she said, Larry began stealing money from the firm and pulled a knife on her in a restaurant.

His horrendous behavior, according to Elisa, began well before Sarah was around—sometime in 1999—and continued until Larry's death. By her own admission, she never did anything more for Larry than help break him out of a rehab. She never once called the police to report his behavior, nor did she turn him in to the California Bar Association, and neither did her best friend, Sarah, or anyone else. Prosecutors believe that's because Elisa lied about the abuse.

Meanwhile, those who loved Larry were having an increasingly difficult time getting in touch with him. Though his son Joe saw him more often than anyone else in the family, Joe began to suspect that Elisa was blocking contact with his father whenever feasible. "You know, she always acted so nice to me," he says, "and then I heard later that she didn't even like me. It was incredible."

Tavia and Cristin had worse experiences when they tried to contact their father. More than five years had passed since Larry and Elisa had hooked up, and Haylei said she never saw either of Larry's daughters. "Tavia was never around," she says. After Sarah's trial, Haylei expressed displeasure and resentment with Tavia's statement before the court, and said that Tavia was hypocritical for coming forward only after Larry's death. Haylei did not know the trials Tavia had gone through, trying to get in touch with her father before he died, or the lengths to which Elisa had gone trying to keep Tavia at arm's length. What was worse, from Tavia's point of view, was that her father would stay with a woman like Elisa.

"She was diagnosed as a pathological liar, my dad

said," Tavia says. "And he hated lying more than anything else. It amazed me that he would stay with a woman like that."

When Elisa was around Joe and Larry, Larry wouldn't even mention his daughters. As soon as Elisa left the room, though, Larry would ask if they were all right and could he do anything to help them. "I can't tell you how many times I tried to figure out why that woman hated me so much," Tavia says.

According to those who were close to the situation, Elisa was like another pop-culture icon, the woman from a Led Zeppelin song, "Dazed and Confused."

"Her soul was created down below," Joe McNabney says.

Tavia says that after her father's murder, she was finally able to figure out why the woman was so nasty and so "dark souled" that she kept women, especially, away from her father. "Now I know why she didn't want me around and why she didn't like having anyone too close. She didn't want anyone figuring out what she was really all about."

Still, with all the manipulation going on, it was hard to see what would drive Elisa, no matter how dark her soul was, to kill Larry when he was the host providing all the nourishment and comfort she so desperately craved.

Elisa later said the catalyst for murdering her husband came at the hotel in Industry City during September 2001. Despite all of Elisa's alleged beatings, the bullet holes in her floor, seeing Larry take numerous drugs and careening around like a pampered rock star, and seeing him with hookers and acting monstrous to her and others, none of that pushed Elisa over the edge. She claimed that on the day she killed Larry, he started drinking at ten a.m. He got so drunk that by mid-afternoon he was disheveled, stumbling and lethargic in the horse show—uncharacteristic for dapper Larry. Then he came back to the hotel room and threatened to kill her dog. That, apparently, was the final straw.

"He took my dog and hung him out on the balcony on the ninth floor and he goes like, 'I'm gonna kill him!' "

He didn't. In fact, he apparently put the dog down, if in fact he ever picked it up, without harming it in any way.

Nevertheless, the incident made more of an impression on Elisa than anything else. Larry could punch her, shoot at her, threaten her with a knife, take heroin, drink profusely, fondle scantily clad hookers, and steal from his own business while busting out of rehab centers, and she could endure all of it. But she had to draw the line of death in the sand when he threatened her dog.

"My dog, I really love my dog," she said.

So, Elisa called Sarah to talk about what they should do to avenge the mistreatment of the dog. The two women felt it would have to be something harsh, because Larry's naked aggression against the helpless canine could not be allowed to stand. He had to die for it, they decided, according to Elisa's confession.

The police, however, were not convinced that a specific incident triggered Sarah and Elisa's murderous fury. It seemed to them that Larry was increasingly isolated and angry, and at the same time, Elisa and Sarah were spending more and more money, draining the bank accounts faster than the money could come into the coffers. Then, months before he was killed, Larry began acting strangely, as if he were drinking heavily. One of the vendors at several horse shows attended by Larry and Elisa told a story that supported the notion that Elisa might slowly be poisoning her husband for much longer than just the weekend before he died.

Vendor Marilyn Mertz said that on August 6, more than month before Larry died, she and Elisa were talking at a horse show about going out for the evening. Elisa, she said, told her that having Larry around would be a drag, and while she didn't mention putting Xylazine in his eyedrops, she did make the infamous comment about spiking his drink. She told Marilyn not to worry about old Larry being a stick in the mud, so "I put a little Vicodin into Larry's wine to put him to sleep."

When questioned, Elisa said she did this because she wanted to gamble with the other vendors, and that would have displeased him. "Go figure," said one of the prosecutors in the aftermath of the investigation. "How could he possibly mind her gambling away what little money he had left?"

Elisa said even more to her, Marilyn Mertz says. She began to ramble and wonder out loud how she could get rid of Larry. When she began working for Larry, he got rid of a previous girlfriend—presumably Elisa was referring to Cheryl Tangen—by giving her a lump sum payment of $150,000. Elisa then asked Marilyn if she had a girlfriend who might be interested in dating Larry so that she could get a $150,000 payoff and just "go away" too.

Trying to sell her husband as a good date, Elisa further told Marilyn that Larry took good care of his girlfriends, that he'd take them to dinner at expensive restaurants and purchase jewels and other items for his lucky paramours. As an afterthought, she said she wanted to ditch Larry because he was beating her. Marilyn didn't notice any marks on Elisa and wondered what type of friend Elisa would be to set someone up with a man who was beating her—not to mention what type of woman would you get for a man who would beat her?

Later, upon hearing Elisa's version of Larry's past, Cheryl Tangen was annoyed. "To say that Larry bought me off is ridiculous," she said. "We remained friendly, talking about meditation and things like that even after we broke up. He never paid me a dime."

While there is no evidence that Larry ever bought off any girlfriend, there is indeed evidence that Larry's murder was a drawn-out affair and not the spontaneous event Elisa and Sarah described afterward.

Two weeks before Larry disappeared, Karen Thompson, another friend on the horse show circuit, was also the recipient of some damning information. She spoke to Elisa about some clothes Elisa was going to sell for her at the horse shows to bring in extra money. After Elisa took the clothes but didn't return with any money, Karen hunted down Larry. He wasn't happy, and told her that Elisa wasn't supposed to be selling clothes—she was supposed to be helping him with the horses.

A few days later Elisa showed up with most of the clothes, and Karen told her, "Hey, I don't want to cause any problems between you and Larry. You don't have to sell these things anymore."

"Don't worry," Elisa told her. "We probably won't even be married by the next horse show."

Karen was scheduled to attend a show on October 4, and by then, as Elisa had said, they weren't married. Larry was dead.

There were other, similar stories. Cheryl Jensen, the landlord for the McNabneys at their Woodbridge, California home, said she met Elisa on August 25 or 26, 2001. Elisa told her, Cheryl said, that her name was Elisa Jordan, that she merely worked for Larry McNabney in his Sacramento law firm, and that Larry was a golf enthusiast looking for a home close to the fairway. Sarah, who was with Elisa at the time, was introduced as her sister, and it was Sarah who was said to be Larry's girlfriend. The only time Cheryl ever met Larry was when he and Elisa signed the lease on the Woodbridge home on August 31, 2001. A few days later the rent check bounced. So it appears that there were some serious money problems in the McNabney law firm even then.

Elisa sent the landlord a new check, and by mid-September that one bounced too. By that time Elisa had Sarah help run interference, to keep the landlord at bay a little longer. It wasn't dissimilar to other things Sarah did for Elisa.

As for Sarah, there was additional evidence that she not only helped kill Larry, but according to some may have been the driving force in his murder. They had a mutual dislike for one another, and Sarah had not hesitated to stand up and talk back to him in ways most employees would never dream of speaking to their bosses. Saying "Fuck you" to Larry at dinner one night not long before his death was noted as an example of the contempt Sarah had for her employer.

What prosecutors and police found fascinating—and revolting—was that for months Elisa and Sarah flaunted their affection for one another, their desire to party at all costs, and their complete disregard for those who could not quench their thirst for instant gratification—and yet no one had been able to put it all together. In fact, if Ginger Miller hadn't come forward, it's unlikely that a case could have been made against them.

After it was all over, Tavia, Joe, and others who loved Larry said they could only see one reason why the vampirelike actions of Elisa and Sarah went unnoticed for so long—it was the state of the nation after September 11.

"Everyone was in shock," Tavia says. "I mean the people on the horse show circuit could've put it together if anyone had ever talked to each other. But the fact was they didn't. These two women walked around draining the life out of everything they touched, and no one put it together until much later. I think everyone was just stunned after the World Trade Center collapsed."

After Larry died, the appetites of the two women, and their behaviors, got worse.

Some saw them as a force of nature. "Like a category five hurricane," said a Florida cop after Elisa was captured.

8

***

A Germ of an Idea

While Sarah and Elisa both maintained that the actual plotting of Larry's death occurred after he had the temerity to threaten to kill Elisa's dog in their Industry City hotel room in the second week of September 2001, the evidence increasingly pointed elsewhere.

Besides the aforementioned events, investigators found other evidence to support the theory that the murder was a gradual event that took on a life of its own as the weeks and months passed.

Spurious comments were made about murder, and specific conversations took place regarding Vicodin, but all of this seemed to be nothing more than idle talk at first. There is little indication that Elisa actually meant to kill Larry when she first came up with the idea. It was a way of letting off steam. She'd encouraged his drinking and his wild behavior. According to former girlfriend Cheryl Tangen, Elisa had presented herself as someone who needed to be rescued, a ploy that also played on Larry's sensibilities, enabling her to manipulate him in any fashion she wanted.

But Elisa appears to have grown tired of the energy it took to maintain her various deceptions. Even after Sarah returned from the exchange student trip overseas during the summer of 2001 and the two of them seriously began considering killing Larry, they vacillated as to whether they would actually carry it out. It was as if they almost backed into his slow poisoning—trying a little to see if they could get away with it, and then gradually upping the dosage until they killed him.

The point of no return snuck up on them quickly. Just a few weeks before Larry went missing, Elisa confronted Debbie Kail in the tack room and asked her if a horse tranquilizer could kill a human being. Debbie, the daughter of horse trainer Greg Whalen, was startled. She told her "of course it would." Anything that would knock out a horse, she said, could have a profound impact on a human being.

In addition, the timing of Haylei's departure to Maine at the end of the summer might have been a premeditated move by Elisa to get her innocent daughter out of the way. Then again, so far as Elisa was concerned, it might have been a lucky coincidence. Whatever the case, Haylei was conveniently not around when Larry turned up missing, and her absence made it that much easier for Sarah and Elisa to plan Larry's death. Or, to put it another way, those who knew both Elisa and Haylei said there was no way Larry would have ended up dead if Haylei had been around.

Elisa apparently thought she had laid the groundwork for committing the crime. Months of telling friends and acquaintances that she had speculated about killing Larry lends credence to her thoughts about it. There are also Elisa's repeated claims of physical abuse, although in the weeks prior to Larry's death, friends who knew both Elisa and Larry said the couple had a fairly normal life together—or at least as routine as it could get for them. No one saw anything that hinted of spousal abuse. That of course raises some doubts about the alleged abuse. It remains impossible to prove Larry McNabney did not beat Elisa, but there is no independent verification for any allegations of abuse and no indication that Elisa ever thought of going to the police at the time. This is one reason investigators would later speculate that the claims were contrived to hide the real motive for Larry's murder.

That possible motive had a lot to do with Sarah Dutra.

Trainer Greg Whalen later testified that he saw Elisa and Sarah emerging from the tack room in the horse quarters at one of the shows, stoned to the gills and giggling like schoolgirls. He thought the two were "thick as thieves," and that Sarah was a bad influence on Elisa. By September 2001, when they finally decided to finish him off, it's now well known that Elisa and Sarah were going through Larry's money like water. Sarah also bragged that she'd even overbilled Elisa, taking advantage of their friendship for money.

On the horse circuit, Larry's friends increasingly saw Elisa and Sarah as inseparable "bovine witches" who not only had the uncontrollable giggles on occasion, but were completely out of control at the sporting events. "You just saw them drunk all the time," said one of the vendors on the circuit. "They always acted like they were plotting something. They kept away from everyone else. They weren't very friendly to us, and they were the two most obnoxious bitches you ever saw in your life."

With many of the same people traveling from venue to venue across the country, the horse circuit is a somewhat closed society. Two women ostracizing themselves from what amounted to a small community stood out, as did their activities. It was hard to overlook the influence of alcohol, marijuana, and worse.

"She was out of control," one of Larry's friends said later of Elisa.

Consequently, Larry went to great lengths to try and explain away his wife's behavior. He also went to great lengths to try and keep up appearances.

In the past, Elisa had attempted to fit in. It was as natural for her as any other deception at which she was adroit. She had always excelled at being part of the crowd, whether it was the cocktail and champagne parties where horse owners wore their best and white-gloved waiters served strawberries and whipped cream, or the trip to the local waffle house with trainers and owners while out on the road trips. Elisa could mesh with any crowd.

But now the veneer was wearing thin. As people got to know her, she couldn't fool them the way she used to, and in the summer of 2001, Larry's friends were beginning to talk about Elisa, saying they thought something was wrong with her. Larry shrugged it off publicly as he had when his son Joe mentioned problems with Elisa. But it must have bothered him. He had to notice that his friends were distancing themselves from Elisa and him.

Now, the subject of Elisa's past became a curiosity. She was extremely vague about it, and her lies had grown more duplicitous. Privately, Larry knew at least something about it. He'd already been reprimanded by the Nevada bar for his wife's past actions, and it made him heartsick, but he couldn't mention it in public without the ramifications boomeranging back on him.

But it is an unanswered question as to how much he knew about Elisa. Relatives remained convinced that if Larry had known the full scope of her background, then he would never have stayed with her. She later said that she'd been brutally honest with Larry and told him everything, and that he had used it against her and made her life a living hell, holding the threat of jail over her head. But such honesty contradicts a lifetime of duplicitous behavior. Her previous husband in Las Vegas, Ken Redelsperger, never knew her real name, for example, so why would she have been more forthcoming with Larry about her Florida criminal record?

It is possible that Elisa was feeling the pinch of that past in the summer of 2001. Her daughter Haylei saw a change in her, and said that at times she felt more like a parent to her own mother because of it, like getting up in the morning to help her get ready for work. Taking care of her mother, whom she idolized, seemed the logical thing for her to do. "My mother was never mean to me," Haylei explained later. "She never spanked me. Not once."

As school began in September, however, Haylei was

in Maine, and Elisa lost her last and best anchor in the real world. Haylei had always been the one who could bring her back down to earth. She knew her mother, probably better than anyone, provided grounding for her, and Elisa had made tremendous concessions to keep Haylei safe, comfortable, and as happy as possible.

In fact, Elisa hated to be alone, and whether it was Haylei or, later, Sarah, Elisa always had someone around her.

Earlier that summer, for instance, when Sarah went on the extended student trip to Italy, was difficult for Elisa. And shortly after Sarah returned, Haylei, who had been around, left for her school in Maine. According to Larry's subsequent autopsy, his long-term poisoning may have begun a short time later.

It was also during this time frame, according to Sarah Dutra's prosecutor, that Larry caught his wife and secretary in bed. Was this mere coincidence, or a motive for Larry's murder? In her confession, Elisa denied that there was anything of a physical nature between her and Sarah. Others agree, or are inclined to believe that if something did happen between the two, it was probably nothing more than experimentation under the influence of drugs. Elisa, just about everyone agrees, liked men.

But prosecutor Tom Testa thinks by the summer of 2001 the relationship between the two women had undergone a fundamental change. Sarah knew that Elisa was her meal ticket, best friend, partner in crime, and the source for the partying Sarah enjoyed immensely. True, both women were very much alike. They were liars, con artists, manipulative, vain, fun-loving spend-thrifts who, liked to party and take life to extremes.

But there was also a basic difference between them: Elisa had been on the run for years, living elaborate lies that were becoming draining. The lies had mounted, the deceptions had gotten larger, and the amount of energy it took to pull off the subterfuge had grown exponentially larger, to the point where Elisa didn't know if she had any energy left in her to give.

Sarah, on the other hand, was younger than Elisa, hadn't traveled as far down the road as Elisa had, or perhaps more accurately, she'd gotten to the same point in the road at a much younger age. Being where Elisa was without as much wear on her, Sarah had the energy, according to the prosecutor, to pull everything off, and therefore became the more dominant of the two. So, according to this line of analysis, if Larry did indeed catch the two in bed together, the idea that he had caught *Sarah* "fucking" his wife may have indicated more than sexual experimentation. Perhaps, as the prosecutor surmised, it also indicated who had control in the relationship.

In Larry's law office, those who saw the two women together concluded that it was indeed Sarah who ran the show, even though Elisa was Sara's employer. Debbie Kail, Greg Whalen's daughter, also saw Sarah at her outlandish worst, telling Larry to go fuck himself the day before he died; again, soon after Sarah's return from Italy. "I think it's pretty obvious they planned [the murder] for a while and started it before Larry actually died," Testa later said.

For Tavia, who was now so far out of her father's life

that she wasn't even sure of Sarah's name, it was a heartbreaking time of loss that got worse after Larry disappeared. For Larry's son Joe, it was a frustrating time because he didn't want to hang around the "hippie chick" Sarah Dutra just to get near his father. Both his father and mother had warned him against spending time alone with Elisa, which by default meant not spending time around her and Sarah, and Joe was only too happy to oblige. He figured that Elisa would get him in a compromising situation if he met her alone, and then lie about it to his father. "I didn't want to get involved in any way with her," Joe says. "I didn't want to give her any reason to say anything to my dad about me, so I stayed away."

With Tavia and Joe—the two children who were most involved in Larry's life—out of the way and effectively neutralized, Elisa and Sarah's bold plan to kill the goose that laid the golden egg took on a life of its own, with much of the timing seemingly determined by Sarah Dutra's activities if not by Sarah herself.

Sarah arrived at the Industry City horse show on Friday, September 7, 2001. Witnesses say that on the following day, Larry wanted her to leave, but she didn't. That led to the confrontation between Sarah and Larry on Sunday, September 9. On Monday, Sarah did leave, to interview the new secretary, Ginger Miller, at the law firm, and she and Elisa spoke by phone that morning, ostensibly talking about Larry's threat on Munchie the dog's life.

Meanwhile, when Sarah was gone, witnesses say Larry was seen walking and talking with friends at the horse show, and appeared in a good mood. Casey Devitt, a fellow horse enthusiast, spent an hour and a half with Larry and said he seemed fine. In fact, those who saw him on the day Sarah left, said he looked as if a weight had been taken from his shoulders.

It wouldn't last long.

Sarah returned at about ten p.m. that night, and Elisa met her outside the hotel, apparently to avoid Larry. Or, alternatively—as police later pointed out—so they could more efficiently plot their next move without the fear of Larry waking up and disturbing them. Whatever the reason, police noted that secret behavior would become the theme for Sarah and Elisa after Larry turned up missing. They planned in secret, met secretly, and kept to themselves.

If Larry was around, Sarah would barely show her face around a horse show. She and Elisa met in tack rooms and skulked around on the fringes of the public display that was central to the shows. They had cajoled, coerced, and intimidated everyone in Larry's life to back off while they plotted to kill him, without anyone actually knowing their plans. Ultimately, this obsessive secrecy made it hard for police to determine exactly who had the idea of killing Larry and who decided to put it into action. "It was largely a circumstantial case," Testa later said about prosecuting Sarah. "We had to use the evidence we had to paint a believable picture, and it was very difficult."

Central to the investigation—and the key to ultimately prosecuting Sarah—was to determine who actually dreamed up, thought out, and executed the plan to kill Larry. "It boiled down to Sarah. We just couldn't see it any other way," says Joe McNabney. All of the McNabney family members saw it the same way, and as a result they found themselves allied with Laren Sims's parents, who believed that Elisa was effectively and deftly manipulated by Sarah Dutra. "If Elisa and Sarah never meet, my dad would be alive today," Tavia says.

The picture the prosecution took pains to paint was of a young, manipulative, and ultimately coldhearted woman, Sarah Dutra, who helped convince the object of her love and affection, Elisa McNabney, that Elisa's husband was evil and needed to be killed. It was no easy task since Elisa was, if nothing else, a practical woman. Why would she want to kill her meal ticket? Her years on the lam had taught her to think a little further than the end of her nose.

In her mid-thirties, Elisa enjoyed instant gratification, but was also growing too weary of her life on the run to sacrifice everything to kill Larry. If Sarah hadn't come along, according to the prosecutors, Elisa would have been content living with Larry for as long as possible, perhaps settling down and taking care of her Florida legal problems through her attorney, Tom Hogan, and eventually leading a seminormal life of luxury with Larry and the horses.

But her past manipulations came back to haunt her. She had manipulated her daughter, and was having problems with her. She had manipulated Larry into partying and imbibing alcohol, and that had gotten away from her too. His infatuation with the "dark side," as Cheryl Tangen called it, had led Larry to Elisa like a moth to an open flame, with similar results. In short, everything Elisa touched "turned to shit," as she supposedly wailed at one point.

Her other problem was Sarah Dutra, over whom Elisa quickly lost control. Sarah, investigators said, began to think that she and Elisa didn't need Larry the meal ticket. She reasoned that they could do it all by themselves: face down anything, run any scam, screw over anyone, and get away with it. Larry was a roadblock to Sarah's desires, and those who investigated the case came to believe that it ultimately became irrelevant who first uttered the words, "Let's kill Larry." To them, there was never any doubt that the one who nurtured that germ of an idea was Sarah Dutra.

"I think Elisa was Sarah's love of her life," detective Deborah Scheffel said. "Not once did Sarah ever show any remorse." But, the prosecutors argued, she did show her love for Elisa by putting the poison in Larry's mouth and volunteering to dig the hole in Yosemite that they both planned to use as Larry's grave. It was only Elisa's concern for the fact that Larry was still alive that kept him from being buried there.

Finally, when it was all said and done, the prosecutors' argument implied, Elisa was outmanipulated by someone who was even more vindictive, ruthless, and callous than she could ever be.

Sarah Dutra won, and Larry was dead.

9

Killing Him Softly

On Sunday night, September 9, 2001, Larry was not himself. By all accounts, he was unhappy and out of sorts. According to some of his friends and acquaintances, he hadn't been himself since Sarah returned from her overseas trip. But no one thought about that until months later.

What they thought about that night was how obnoxious Larry had become. Drinking heavily at dinner, he'd put off his friends and acquaintances, and some of them were concerned. They knew he had a history of drinking, and thought it would be a terrible personal tragedy if Larry sacrificed all those years of sobriety just to fall off the wagon now.

Perhaps it was the liquor that caused his mood swings that night, or it could have been the effect of liquor and the horse tranquilizer that prosecutors believe Elisa and Sarah were slowly administering to him during the previous weeks.

Debbie Kail, Greg Whalen's daughter, remembered that as they all sat down for dinner that Sunday night, Larry became agitated. He even called her a bitch, in front of the rest of the table. She said it wasn't like him to drink and be mean or rude.

Larry's outburst seemed mild in comparison to what happened next. He saw Sarah at the table and got upset with her presence. She had invaded the sanctity of his quarter horse getaways. He didn't like her there, and bluntly told her so.

She responded in an equally caustic manner.

"Fuck you, Larry," she said.

The table was taken aback. Debbie thought it was particularly provocative, considering that Larry was Sarah's boss.

The next morning, September 10, 2001, Debbie said Larry showed up at the horse show looking very strange. He was not the dapper, well-dressed man she always remembered seeing. He was rumpled and wearing wrinkled pants, his shirt not even buttoned correctly. He had never shown himself in public in such a fashion. It was an anathema to him to be seen in such a condition. So Debbie suggested he change his clothes. At first, he didn't seem to realize what she was talking about. That was odd as well, she thought. No matter how much Larry partied, he was always focused enough to know what was going on, and he was always well-dressed at professional competitions, where dress and style were everything. It was the only time in his life anyone associated with him in the quarter horse circuit ever saw him off his game. Debbie couldn't figure out why.

Later that morning, Larry brought his horse out for showing. Again, he didn't seem to be himself. He didn't seem to know the routine he and his horse would go through, although he'd practiced it dozens of times before and had never made a mistake. He seemed confused, lethargic, and distant. Others noticed, and some thought he was falling into old patterns and had begun to drink heavily. A few expressed surprise, because Larry usually liked to show himself off as much as his horses. And then there were those like Greg Whalen, who worried, and who wondered what was wrong with his good friend.

Larry's behavior that morning was in stark contrast to how he appeared a little bit later. According to several witnesses, he looked very happy. The abrupt mood swings certainly could have indicated poisoning, the result of which might well have manifested itself in even stranger behavior later that evening.

That night, Larry said he didn't feel like going to dinner and was going to stay in his hotel room. It was extremely odd behavior for him. Usually when he went on the road with his horse trainer and friends, they had dinner and drinks together. It was one of the little rituals of comradery that he had enjoyed in the past on his horse show trips. It didn't seem right to Greg Whalen, who was now even more worried about Larry than he had been that morning. He thought that perhaps Larry was sick. When Greg called him in his hotel room and asked if he wanted some soup sent to him, Larry was uncharacteristically abrupt. He sounded drunk and mumbled something about not wanting "any damn soup" before he hung up. This outburst was also out of character for Larry, because he not only saw Greg Whalen as a friend, but as a mentor and a confidant. He wouldn't normally react that way to Greg's show of concern—or for that matter, to anyone who showed him kindness.

Shortly after six-thirty p.m., Elisa came downstairs, where Greg and his daughter were dining at the Putter Cup restaurant. She ordered a bowl of soup, a drink for herself, and two goblets of Chardonnay, saying they were for Larry. She complained about Larry being drunk all the time and said she was tired of picking up after him. Debbie knew that in the last couple of weeks Elisa had voiced similar complaints, but until the Industry City horse show, she hadn't observed anything but good relations between the two.

Of course, nothing was all right between the two, and while Elisa was downstairs voicing her complaints about Larry, Sarah was upstairs in the hotel room, tending to the murder.

Sarah did not start the day with Elisa and Larry. She began it at the law firm, breaking in the new secretary. Ginger Miller said she remembered that September 10, 2001, her first day on the job for the McNabney firm, because it was the day before the World Trade Center attacks. She came to work early, as she usually liked to do on a job, only to wait an hour and a half because no one was there to open up the office. Concerned, she called her family to see if her new employer had left her a message. No one had. "I guess Elisa and Larry were in L.A. at a horse show, so Sarah was running late," Ginger later told police. "I think [Sarah] called and talked to Elisa, and Elisa said that she was going to be stuck a little bit longer and for me to come back on Wednesday, and she would pay me for these days and she was sorry."

According to her later confession, Elisa offered two versions of what she did that day. She was busy talking to Sarah about the murder plans or, alternately, crying about the attempted murder of her dog, Munchie.

According to Ginger, Sarah overslept that day. "She was supposed to give me paperwork and stuff, and I asked her if I was supposed to have some kind of contract or paperwork, and she said not to worry about that, they would give it to me later. She told me to take these forms home that our clients are supposed to sign and read them and go over them so I know what to do for the job. That's the only training that they gave me."

She left and came back on Wednesday, completely unaware of what was actually going on in the firm. "Elisa said Sarah should just show me around and that was it," Ginger says. The telephone call from Elisa about her beloved Munchie spurred Sarah, a devout dog lover, to drop everything and quickly fly to Industry City, outside of Los Angeles, where she then took a cab to the hotel.

When she got to the room, Larry was already asleep and there were no signs of violence against Munchie. In fact, the double room was quite tidy, and Sarah and Elisa kept it that way. They quietly sat on the empty bed across from Larry as he slept soundly in the other bed. That's when the conversation supposedly turned deadly, from idle speculation between the two women about killing Larry, to actually committing the murder. Investigators who believe the two had slowly poisoned

Larry over a longer period of time say that in the hotel room they finally decided to finish him off.

Whatever the case, they didn't make a move on Larry at first. They decided to plan the murder on the spur of the moment. The key was getting the horse tranquilizer and administering it to Larry. Finally, they both got up the nerve to go down to the trainer's trailer and get the poison.

It made Elisa very nervous. They actually were going to go through with it. They were going to kill Larry. She and Sarah were at the point of no return, and then gladly stepped across the threshold.

Deciding that the best way to administer the poison was orally, Elisa and Sarah devised a method of putting horse tranquilizer in an eyedrop bottle and slowly squeezing drops into Larry's mouth as he slept.

Elisa was so nervous that she couldn't administer the poison effectively while Larry dozed. So it fell to Sarah Dutra to do it. While Sarah later said she was scared to death of Elisa, and in fact used that as a defense in her trial, she never left or called the police. Nor did she flee later, when she had the chance, and in fact she was seen several times after Larry's death, hanging out and partying with Elisa.

According to the prosecutors, Sarah took control on that day. Greg Whalen later told police that Larry had told him in recent weeks that he wanted to fire Sarah. "I could see that it was coming to a head," he recalled. But it would be Sarah, who had flipped Larry off at dinner the night before, who would bring it to a head.

According to one of the stories Sarah later told, she got to the hotel on September 10, after the interview with Ginger Miller at the offices in Sacramento. When she got to the horse show, Elisa told her she had already begun to poison Larry. This is where Elisa claimed Sarah helped her, but Sarah claimed at first that she did not. After midnight, she did admit she went into the hotel room and checked on Larry and that he was still alive.

The next day, Sarah admitted to riding around with Elisa, looking for a wheelchair. In a scene that sounded like it came out of a Quentin Tarantino film, the two women first stopped at a hospital and Elisa ran inside to see if she could liberate a wheelchair. When that didn't work, they stopped at a Wal-Mart, and eventually a Target. They were unsuccessful. Then they got the idea to find a place to rent the wheelchair, and when they found one, Sarah admitted that she freely went with her friend to procure it. She gave her ID to Elisa—since Elisa didn't have one of her own—so she could rent the chair. Sarah even paid for it herself, and opened the door of the store as Elisa wheeled it out.

It was Sarah who put the wheelchair in the back of the truck, then helped push Larry into the vehicle using the wheelchair once they got back to the hotel.

The next morning, as the nation was stunned and beginning to mourn the loss of lives at the World Trade Center's twin towers, Elisa showed up at Debbie Kail's room with Sarah and, proceeding to trade in on the collective grief of the nation, told Debbie that she and Larry had a fight the previous evening and that Larry left her. Sarah had flown down to comfort her, she said, because she was such a good secretary and friend, and was concerned about the grief Larry was causing her.

A little while later, when Elisa again saw Debbie, she told her that she had spoken with Larry by cell phone and he was in Florida. Debbie frowned at that, said she had tried to call Larry's cell phone to see if he was all right and had been unable to reach him. Elisa then told Debbie that she had Larry's cell phone *with her*. All Debbie could do was scratch her head and wonder how Elisa could reach Larry by cell if she had the phone with her.

It wasn't the only odd behavior Debbie had seen from Elisa recently. When they were grooming horses together a few weeks earlier, Elisa had asked Debbie about horse tranquilizers. She wanted to know what a horse tranquilizer that could knock out a 1,500-pound horse could do to a 200-pound man. On the day Larry disappeared, Debbie didn't immediately connect the dots.

No one else who saw strange goings-on that day made the connection either.

Debbie did think it strange when she saw a Do Not Disturb sign on Larry's hotel room later that morning. He usually liked to get up early on the road. She looked outside and saw Larry's red pickup truck with Elisa's dog inside. This struck her as strange, since the hotel allowed pets. Even stranger was what Debbie saw in the back of the truck: bags containing what appeared to be dirty laundry, two shovels, and a wheelchair. When she saw Elisa, she was told that the wheelchair was part of Sarah Dutra's school project. Sarah painted surrealistic paintings, which also struck an odd chord with Debbie. "What the hell would she do with a wheelchair?" Debbie later asked. "That didn't fit."

A little while later, Debbie and her father, Greg Whalen, went to their horse trailer, where all the show gear was kept. Larry's boots, hats, and clothes were gone. Elisa's straw show hat was found under the trailer. Another trainer in the area later told Debbie that Elisa had offered him Larry's ostrich-skin boots, hats, and clothes.

"Won't Larry need this stuff?" the trainer had asked.

"Larry isn't going to need these," Elisa had replied. "He is never coming back. He'll never show horses again."

Elisa said Larry had left her, but she didn't explain why he suddenly wouldn't need his clothes. Presumably, even if he left her, he'd still need to dress.

Debbie saw Elisa again after breakfast, still early in the morning, and Elisa told her she was going back to see if Larry had cleaned out their account, meaning that she was going to leave the horse show and drive back to Sacramento. She didn't return until the next afternoon, and when Debbie said she was starting to worry about her, Elisa told her she'd gone to Sacramento to check on some papers at the law office.

The wheelchair was still in the back of the truck, and it had a story to tell.

After wheeling Larry out of the hotel the previous day, Elisa and Sarah had taken him to Yosemite for a discreet burial.

According to testimony in Sarah's subsequent trial,

Sarah did most of the driving up to Yosemite, since she knew the way, having gone there many times as a child. She also remembered Larry's semiconscious threat about her and Elisa not getting away with the murder, and she remembered Elisa coldly removing Larry's expensive Rolex from his wrist.

Did she ever show any signs of concern, or did she call the police, or even once ask how Larry was doing? No. Instead, she stopped along the way, got out of the car, pumped some gas and had a cigarette and a quick snack. When they got to Yosemite, it was Sarah who popped out of the car with the shovel and tried to dig a hole. She pronounced the ground "too rocky," although Elisa said she didn't want to bury Larry because he was still alive. It made more sense, Elisa said, to go home and let him die, that burying people alive is much more difficult. But Sarah didn't care. She probably would have been just as happy to bury him then and there. What's more the only time she voiced any concern about anything during the trip was when she got upset about her dog being alone while they were busy killing Larry.

When they later reached the McNabney home, Sarah left to take an extended forty-five-minute ride to retrieve her dog Ralphie, so it would be safe. She never called the police or poison control, nor did she ever show the slightest concern for Larry McNabney.

According to Greg Whalen, Elisa and Sarah didn't show any outward sign of concern for Larry on September 11 either, or when they returned to the horse show the next day with the wheelchair still propped up in the back of the pickup truck.

Greg said on the morning of September 11 at about

five a.m., he noticed Elisa's hat under the trailer. The shovels at that point were inside the horse trailer, while Larry's bag of boots and clothes were not. About an hour and a half later Elisa approached him and told him that Larry had left and that Greg shouldn't get Larry's horse ready to show because he had decided not to show horses ever again.

"Oh, and by the way, do you know anyone who wants to buy Larry's truck?" she asked.

As a matter of fact, Greg did. Casey Devitt was interested. He was a horse trainer who knew the McNabneys fairly well and he was among those present at the horse show. Debbie Kail told him that Elisa said Larry had left the horse show to join a cult, and she was interested in selling their pickup.

When Casey got to the show on September 12, he tendered a $27,000 offer, well below the going rate for the truck, but Elisa was eager to accept it. She reiterated the story that Larry had joined a cult and said he was "much happier now." Casey, though, noticed that Elisa was wearing Larry's favorite Rolex watch, and that his horseshoe-shaped ring, a favorite of his, was on a necklace around her neck. He grimaced at that, wondering what to think. Then Elisa volunteered that Larry would no longer need his worldly possessions, asked Casey his boot size, and said that Larry would want him to have his boots and shirts.

"I thought that was a bit odd," he told police later. "Even if he wasn't going to show horses anymore, he'd still want to wear clothes."

"Believe me, where he's at, he'll never want these again," Elisa explained.

In retrospect, prosecutors were amazed that Elisa and Sarah were able to pull it off. They were as brazen and as arrogant in killing Larry as possible. They practically told everyone that they'd whacked him, but no one could actually believe that two beautiful women with seemingly everything going for them could execute such a cold, calculated murder.

They very nearly didn't.

At first the prosecutors had no idea how the murder had occurred, even as they suspected that Elisa and Sarah had plotted Larry's death. When they came to know the gruesome details, veteran police investigators were shocked.

It was hard for some of them to imagine a more nightmarish murder, tortuous and strung out over such a long period of time.

While hanging on a hook in a chemical-induced state of lethargy, Larry knew he was dying and could do *nothing* about it. The two women who coldly murdered him never once tried to help him or showed even the slightest concern about him.

He was a bug to be crushed, and once they were rid of him, Elisa and Sarah divided up his cherished possessions, laughed at his misfortune, and continued to desecrate his memory for several months after they'd killed him.

As for Larry, his victimization only began with his death. The worst was still to come.

10

In the Cooler

By the time Elisa and Sarah got Larry home on the night of September 11, there was little that could be done for him, even if they were inclined to do so. There was even some speculation among the police that Larry didn't die at home, but expired either in his hotel room or somewhere along the meandering ten-hour drive first to Yosemite from Industry City and then to the Woodbridge home in Sacramento.

The most compelling evidence that Larry did not die in Industry City is the fact that they took him home without burying him. It is one of the few independently verifiable facts that backs up Elisa's assertions that Larry fought for his life until the bitter end, and is one of the few pieces of testimony offered by Sarah or Elisa about Larry's death that is uncontested by the two of them. Both seemed to agree that Larry wouldn't die as he stumbled around his hotel room and fought them in the truck. They also agreed that they finally had to take him home while he was still alive because they didn't know what else to do with him.

What happened next varies greatly depending upon whom you wish to believe.

Sarah claimed she didn't even know what happened the day Larry died. Though she at first admitted that she was at the horse show the day Larry was poisoned, she said she never saw anything suspicious. She claimed that the last time she saw Larry was at the show. According to that first story, Elisa and Larry appeared to be getting along, but Elisa told her that Larry was doing heroin and "any drugs he could get his hands on." Sarah, though, said she only saw Larry drinking. Later, when questioned by police, she altered her story a bit and said she saw Elisa push Larry into the pickup truck on a wheelchair.

Elisa asked to borrow Sarah's credit card to rent the wheelchair so she could get Larry out of the hotel before he made an ass of himself, Sarah said. She also said Larry seemed dazed and was swinging his arms around and acting wildly. Elisa responded by telling Larry to calm down, then told her that Larry had fought with her the night before and had kicked her so hard she could barely walk. So, according to Sarah, Elisa had spent the night sleeping in the truck.

Sarah finally admitted to going with Elisa as they drove Larry north, ultimately to his Woodbridge home via the aborted Yosemite burial. She said she couldn't miss the obvious and sensed something was horribly wrong with Larry. Perhaps it was the white spittle hanging off the edge of his mouth, or that he was screaming that she and Elisa would never get away with murder—but Sarah merely said she picked up on something as she helped her friend Elisa and drove the red pickup north. Larry was sprawled in the backseat moaning as he was dying, and Sarah couldn't help but notice it.

She said she questioned Elisa more than once about what was going on. "This is kind of scaring me, Elisa. What's going on?" she claimed she asked.

"You need to forget that you ever saw Larry today," Elisa supposedly told her.

Sarah claimed she woke the next morning after sleeping in the downstairs living room of the McNabney home and was immediately summoned upstairs to Larry and Elisa's bedroom. "She told me to come upstairs. That's when I saw him," she said.

According to Sarah, Elisa seemed almost pleased with her kill as she stepped into the hall and summoned Sarah to come upstairs and gaze upon the horrific results of her activity from the night before. According to Sarah, it was a scene faintly reminiscent of an Anne Rice novel.

"Her eyes were big," Sarah claimed, and Elisa shot her a "threatening look," and she "felt paralyzed" in Elisa's hypnotic grasp. "I thought she was reading my mind," Sarah cried in anguish. "She was twisted."

For fans of melodrama, it doesn't end there. "She looked evil," Sarah said, bemoaning her fate as she was drawn up the stairs to where Elisa stood with her trophy. "I was scared . . . It felt like I had a chain around my neck that she was holding . . ."

With stern words of warning, Elisa found her voice and cried, "If you care about yourself, you will forget about this." In response, Sarah was barely able to contain herself, since she'd never seen a dead body before.

"Larry is dead," Elisa said calmly.

Sarah freaked out. "What do you mean Larry's dead?" she exclaimed, apparently terrified. That's when her sense of moral indignity kicked in. "Oh my God, we've got to go to the police," she claimed she told Elisa.

But Elisa was controlling events and would have none of that. "She said going to the police was the last thing I wanted to do," Sarah claimed, and said Elisa told her, "You go to the police you'll end up just like him."

Sarah said she was unaware of how Larry died, citing either alcohol or drugs as the most likely candidates for agents in his death. According to her that's when the bizarre got macabre. Elisa forced her into helping haul Larry's dead body downstairs and into the garage refrigerator. Sarah said she told her no at first, but Elisa was adamant and wouldn't take no for an answer. Finally, Sarah said she was too weak to resist Elisa's evil intentions and found herself almost in a dream, helping to schlep the dead body downstairs.

"She said, 'You're going to help me put the body in the refrigerator,'" Elisa allegedly told her.

"I can't do this," Sarah replied.

Elisa said, "You have no choice. It is in your best interest to do exactly what I say."

So Sarah helped Elisa. "From there, I don't remember anything," she concluded.

But apparently she did remember more, and went on to say that Elisa removed a sheet from the bed and spread it on the floor. They both wrapped the body in the sheet as if it were a burial shroud, and after Elisa had taken a blanket from the bed, they wrapped him in that too. Afterward, Sarah helped carry the body downstairs and dutifully cleared out shelves in the refrigerator. The two women then folded Larry up enough to stuff him inside. Then Elisa told Sarah to get herself together, that she would go back to the office and pretend that nothing had happened.

"I felt like a dog on a leash," Sarah said. "Like I had to do what she said. She told me I could go to prison for what I did. I felt horrible. I didn't go to the police because I was afraid of her."

But that wasn't all. Sarah said Elisa was able to coerce her into keeping her mouth shut because Elisa told her she had friends in low places. "I was afraid of her and the people that she knew. When she told me to worry about my family, I said, 'Oh God!' " Sarah claimed.

After Elisa lectured her and left, she thought she had a chance to reflect on what had happened, but had seriously underestimated the horror of having a dead body in the refrigerator. She couldn't help but walk back downstairs, she said, and look in the refrigerator to see if Larry was actually dead. As she crept slowly down the hall and finally into the garage, she found her heart was racing. She couldn't believe she'd been involved in something so heinous. She was feeling numb with guilt and fear, and said she could have screamed at the drop of a hat.

She was, after all, in a home alone with a dead man.

So, according to Sarah, she opened the basement door and saw that the refrigerator door was open!

This revelation raised goose bumps even before she saw that Larry McNabney, or at least some portion of his body, was sticking out of the refrigerator door.

She freaked out again. The image of Larry, folded up in a sheet and a blanket, with an imagined blank expression on his face and his hand sticking out of the refrigerator, would haunt her for months. At first she thought he was alive, so she gathered enough courage to check and see.

But Laurence William McNabney was still dead. His body, merely in a state of rigor mortis, had stiffened and forced the refrigerator door open. Naturally panicked by this, Sarah did the first thing that came to mind. She stuffed Larry back inside and secured the door by wrapping duct tape around the refrigerator several times so Larry couldn't open it again.

Later, Sarah ditched the idea of spending any time at the office and decided to rejoin Elisa, who had returned to the horse show. She testified that she was so terrified of Elisa that even when she had the opportunity to run or call the cops, she felt powerless against Elisa's hypnotic spell. She had to do whatever Elisa wanted. So she got into the Saab that Elisa had bought her and headed down the highway at breakneck speed to catch up with her.

The college junior may have had a lot of talent, but driving a car like the wind after seeing a dead body in a refrigerator wasn't one of them. She totaled the car in her haste to leave the confines of the Woodbridge home. She only made it into Elisa's loving and understanding arms after renting a car to get back to Industry City.

Elisa's story resembles Sarah's story only in the fact that at the end of it Larry was dead in a refrigerator in the garage. Otherwise, it's a different script, with the same essential actors and a different director.

In Elisa's director's cut, it was Sarah who had gained control that day. She kept Elisa calm when Elisa wanted to panic. In the truck, when Elisa saw white stuff coming out of Larry's mouth, she almost lost it, but Sarah stroked her arm and told her it was going to be okay. Elisa said Sarah always seemed to have the ability calm her down whenever she got upset.

In Sarah's version, she drove because she was forced to, but in Elisa's version it was symbolic of the control Sarah had over events. Sarah drove. Sarah was in control. Even so, Elisa didn't absolve herself of all guilt. She confessed to doing some fairly horrific things. She admitted that when they got home that night, Larry was still alive. She took off his clothes and bathed him, then put him in some clean boxers and a T-shirt. Those items would be the last ones Larry would wear.

Elisa also said she was guilty of discussing options with Sarah as to what they should do if Larry came out of his stoned stupor and was a vegetable or worse.

According to Elisa, there was no drama the next morning when she and Sarah awoke. They sat watching the television morning news shows and the continuing coverage of the 9/11 tragedy, and almost as an afterthought both of them looked in on Larry and found him dead on the floor.

As for storing the body in the cooler, she claimed that Sarah was a willing and able conspirator, although her description of sheet wrappings and carrying the body downstairs doesn't deviate too much from Sarah's.

"I wanted to kill him . . . Sarah wanted to kill him," she told police.

According to Elisa, Larry was jealous of Sarah and Haylei. "He was jealous of my horse trainer, who's seventy. He was jealous of Sarah. He was jealous . . . he was jealous because . . . he didn't like me to have anybody outside," Elisa said.

The stories of the two women begin to converge again as they discussed what happened to them on September 12. On that day, Sarah wrecked the Saab in her haste to flee the dead body in the refrigerator, and Elisa went back to the horse show to establish an alibi by hanging out with the horses. On Wednesday, Elisa and Sarah returned to Larry's offices in Sacramento. Since he'd been reprimanded before the Nevada bar, Larry's only remaining office was in Sacramento, and the only people left working for him were Elisa and occasionally Haylei and Sarah. Everything was going to change now that Elisa and Sarah had killed Larry and were firmly in charge of the law firm. No one was going to do any of the work, if they could avoid it, except the new girl on the scene, Ginger Miller. With Larry out of the way, Sarah and Elisa were going to exploit the worker, steal the cash, and run the business into the ground.

On the road to Perdition, they were going to ruin a few more lives, tie up dozens of police and investigators, cause chaos and pandemonium among those in the quarter horse community—not to mention the lives of their respective families—and throw caution to the wind in an effort to outrun the consequences of Larry's murder.

Ultimately they couldn't do it, but it wouldn't keep them from trying.

It started as soon as they got back to Sacramento. Larry was on ice and the show was about to begin.

11

Hungry Mouths Talk

It's almost impossible to figure out many of the details of Larry's death, not only because he and his wife are dead, but because when Elisa was alive and hanging out with Sarah, the two of them lied about so many things and so often that even the most mundane facts are questionable.

Take, for example, Cheryl Jensen, the landlord of the home in Woodbridge. It was a nice neighborhood, exclusive, just off of a golf course where Larry liked to play. By mid-September Elisa had bounced two checks to the woman, but Elisa kept playing with her.

At first Elisa told Cheryl the reason why her check bounced was that an employee from the law firm had stolen a stack of checks. When the second check bounced, Cheryl got Elisa on the telephone, and Elisa told her that the checks kept bouncing because Larry had a neurological incident like a stroke and he couldn't be moved for a few weeks. There was a great doctor in St. Louis, according to Elisa, and by golly she was going to get her husband there to save him.

What Larry's neurological event had to do with Elisa bouncing checks, Elisa didn't say. What happened to the employee who stole a stack of checks? Elisa didn't say.

The story doesn't end there. Elisa told Cheryl that Larry was so bad off he couldn't even speak, which actually was the truth, but according to Elisa it wasn't because he was dead. He'd just had a horrible stroke and he was using a computer to communicate. This placated Cheryl for a few more days, but it didn't make her forget that the McNabneys owed her money. On September 22, 2001, she posted a pay or leave notice at the house. When she got home, there was a phone message from Elisa. There were more excuses. The reason she hadn't been in contact, Elisa said, was because she was in a car accident and lost her cell phone.

The lies cascaded out of Elisa's mouth like sewer water out of a punctured septic tank. The worst of it started the day she and Sarah killed Larry. As police began to unravel the mystery, they soon found themselves happy they didn't have to rely on the words of either Sarah or Elisa in deciphering what had happened. They had Ginger, the newest secretary in the McNabney law firm, to help them figure it out.

Ginger Miller, a pretty blonde who wanted to do charity work, unknowingly got a ringside seat to the Theatre of the Absurd production in the McNabney law office following Larry's murder. When she returned to work two days after her aborted first day on the job, Larry was dead and Sarah and Elisa were running things. All Ginger knew from the first day was that it was the strangest office in which she'd ever worked.

When she first spoke with Elisa, Ginger got a quick slap in the face regarding her tenure in the firm. "I smoke dope and my daughter doesn't know it. And she smokes dope and thinks I don't know. I also don't like niggers. If that bothers you, then you can find someplace else to work," Elisa told Ginger.

Ginger was taken aback by her boss's proclamation and repulsed by some of the other behavior she saw around the office. But she also found herself charmed by Elisa, Sarah, and even Haylei, because the women who worked in the office were all physically attractive, full of energy, and at times very friendly.

"I don't know how to put it, but they all treated me nicely," Ginger says. "At least in the beginning they did. I've worked in offices where everyone treats you like crap because you're good-looking. But it wasn't that way with Elisa and Sarah. It was a breath of fresh air."

She enjoyed the company of Haylei as much as that of Sarah and Elisa, and remembered going shopping with her and even introducing Haylei to her family. "I remember that Halloween after Larry died, Elisa had me take Haylei and go out shopping instead of coming into work," Ginger says.

In another office it might be strange to take a day off in order to go shopping with the boss's child, but in the McNabney firm, strange was a relative term.

The attractive, former exotic dancer was originally hired because Elisa liked her looks. "Elisa told me she only wanted to have good-looking girls working in the office," Ginger explains. "She and Sarah were very much into appearances."

Ginger often found her new bosses twittering in the office, talking about casual flings, boyfriends, and makeup. "They would talk about one boyfriend Sarah had . . . and they'd make fun of him and every other man."

Inside the firm, the three women became fast friends, and when Haylei got back into town before Halloween, they found themselves kidding each other that they were "Charlie's Angels."

"I was the Lucy Liu character," Ginger explains. "Haylei was Drew Barrymore because she dressed like Drew and had that kickass attitude. Sarah was Cameron Diaz, and we named Elisa Charlie because Charlie should've been a woman anyway."

Ginger thought at first she'd found a fine home inside the McNabney firm, though the offices were unkempt and Elisa could be strident about making sure that no clients ever came to the office. "She was all about getting new clients and wining and dining them. She never wanted them to come back to our office."

A petite blonde with full lips and almond-shaped eyes, Ginger dressed and looked like a Hollywood actress—which she aspired to be.

Elisa and Sarah both spent money as quickly as they could on their personal appearance. "I remember she showed me a picture of her with her husband Larry, and she said, 'Here's Botox and detox,'" Ginger says.

It seemed that at least once a week Elisa was getting

Botox injections, while Sarah frivolously spent money on clothes.

Naturally, Ginger was curious about the man whose name was on the door. Where was Larry? The first week she was in the law firm, Elisa told her that Larry had gone to an enjoyable men's retreat and would be back soon. Elisa described how Larry was overworked and needed the rest and how much better he would be and how refreshed he would seem when he returned. Ginger shrugged it off and at first didn't think much about the boss not being around. Nothing seemed overly suspicious at that point, at least nothing that would point to foul play. The office just seemed, for a lack of a better term, *weird*.

Still, after a while it bothered Ginger that Larry never appeared. She asked when she was going to meet him and was told different things at different times. For Elisa and Sarah, for whom a deceptive nature was secondary, fooling everyone about Larry's whereabouts became a game that they loved to play.

First, he was out of town on business, and later he was golfing. One day Ginger was told she had just missed him by a mere five minutes. Taking a cue from the movie *Nine to Five*, Sarah and Elisa concocted elaborate schemes to convince everyone that Larry was still alive and kicking, when all the while he was folded up next to the vegetables in the refrigerator.

He had joined a cult to seek enlightenment. He had gone on a drinking binge. He'd traveled to Europe or was away on the golf course somewhere. Each of these were elaborate lies told at various times by Elisa and Sarah when the mood struck them. The lies took on lives of their own as the two produced episodes of the *Where's Larry?* show for the small audience of friends and family who needed to be kept at bay until Elisa fled the state. Ginger Miller said that the only excuse she didn't hear was that Larry was on the space shuttle.

From September until the end of November, Ginger came to work every day, often beating her employers to the office, and she stayed late and did whatever menial work was assigned to her. But she was never satisfied with the answers she got about Larry's whereabouts, or more precisely, what answers she *didn't* get about his whereabouts. By the end of November she was very suspicious of Elisa, Sarah, and even Haylei.

She certainly got off to an odd enough start. She got paid for an entire week of work, though she didn't actually work it. That's because her first day was September 10, 2001, and on that day Elisa and Sarah had their hands full killing Larry, so they couldn't spend time in the office with a new secretary. So they just paid her for work she didn't do. They may have been murderers, but they didn't want to offend their new employee, or more precisely, they didn't want to chase away the only worker bee they had left. According to Ginger, that's why Sarah, who had overslept and showed up late, looking scraggily, told her to come back in a few days.

At the time, Sarah and Elisa literally had their hands filled with Larry, and even two days later they were so shaken up by what they'd done that Elisa called Ginger and told her to take the rest of the week off. Naturally, Elisa didn't tell her the truth. She merely told Ginger that she was still stuck at the horse show in L.A. because of the World Trade Center tragedy. "The horse show was taking a little longer than expected because of the war" was the way Ginger said Elisa explained the situation. "But that morning when she told me that I could have the rest of the week off, she did sound very happy."

When Ginger did see the two again, she found out about Sarah wrecking the Saab, but not, of course, that it was because Sarah was disturbed over seeing Larry's dead body sticking out of the refrigerator. The story Ginger got was less horrific, but at least as dramatic. According to Sarah, she had been cruising down to L.A. when the brakes suddenly failed. Thrust into a perilous situation and perhaps facing her own death, the heroic Sarah had stoically imitated James Garner in countless episodes of *The Rockford Files* and ran the car aground, swerving to avoid plunging over cliffs and avoiding cars in the process—all while going seventy miles per hour.

But, of course, they couldn't tell the insurance company that Sarah was driving the Saab. In order to collect the insurance, Elisa claimed she was driving. Amazingly, she did this while not in possession of a California driver's license.

Ginger's introduction to the Larry McNabney law firm with Elisa and Sarah presiding was, as with everything else regarding them, not as it was supposed to be. On Monday, September 17, the first day she did in fact work, Ginger was a half hour early and Sarah and Elisa showed up together about ten minutes late. "That was starting to irk me already," Ginger says. "As soon as I got a key I knew it wouldn't be an issue. They were pretty much late every day."

And, according to Ginger, both women showed up together about ninety percent of the time. But apparently neither one of them had been doing much work. They spent Ginger's first week showing her the ropes, how to file papers and answer phones, and while it was all interesting work for Ginger, who, like Elisa, had once worked for a chiropractor as an office manager, she was put off with the sheer *amount* of work she was going to be forced to do. She wasn't one to shy away from a challenge, but noticed right away that none of the office paperwork had been done since July.

"All the paperwork just stopped," she recalls. "All the payments sent out and all kinds of lost messages and checks were in July. It seemed like no one did any work in August at all."

Elisa was a slob, she thought, and always late to work, as was Sarah, and the necessary legal work hadn't been done in the firm for a while, but that only smacked of laziness, not criminal activity. It did seem, however, very unprofessional for a lawyer's office. Its unkempt appearance and the cavalier attitude of the two women in the office left Ginger wondering what was going on. When Elisa and Sarah both said they'd initially been hired as secretaries for the small firm, Ginger couldn't help but wonder what the women were getting paid for, since none of the work seemed to get done.

Then, at the end of the month, another character entered the office—Haylei, Elisa's daughter. Elisa told

Ginger that Haylei was an emancipated minor who had been at a horse school on the East Coast, and while that seemed to add up, Ginger was by now suspicious because of Elisa's other explanations and activities.

In fact, Ginger knew that Elisa "lied about everything," and that put her on guard. She also noticed that Elisa and Haylei often argued and that it appeared that Elisa didn't want her daughter around. "I think Elisa pushed her aside a long time ago," Ginger later explained.

A few days after Ginger started with the firm she got a brand new episode of *Where's Larry?* from Elisa. In this latest episode, Larry was drunk and struggling to sober up out there in the big cruel world. This was one of the stories Haylei heard too, according to Ginger. One day Ginger said Elisa asked to speak with her for a moment. "She comes down and tells me that she really didn't want to talk about this, but that she should probably share it with me now," Ginger recalls. "She said that Larry had a drinking problem and he's been an alcoholic for years and has been in and out of clinics all his life. She said this is the one, though, that he was going to clean up. She said he was off in Oregon or Washington or something, apparently at this clinic."

Meanwhile, Elisa had other stories for people in Larry's life. She'd already told horse trainers within the first few days of his disappearance that he'd joined a cult. Toward the end of September she began to tell everyone that she and Larry had divorced.

Ginger soon saw her and Sarah hanging around one of Larry's friends, Rick, who had a lot of money. He had been close to Larry for several years. Ginger was under the impression that he was a very good friend of Larry's who'd been told the same story of alcoholism that Elisa first told her. Rick bought it, according to Ginger, because he knew Larry had struggled with a drinking problem in the past.

Soon Rick was offering a comforting shoulder for Elisa, thinking he was helping the wife of a friend who needed consoling. Then that apparently became something else, and when Elisa came back from a weekend with Rick, Ginger saw something that she later attributed to a rush of grief and guilt coming from Elisa. At the time, she didn't know what to make of it.

One day, as Ginger and Elisa found themselves alone in the office, Elisa began to complain bitterly about Larry. Then suddenly she broke down into huge rasping sobs. Ginger said she was inconsolable and almost uncontrollable. This went on for a while, and Ginger could tell that Elisa was deeply troubled about something, but at the time she didn't know what it was.

All she knew was that things weren't adding up. Besides the sob fest, within a month of going to work at the McNabney law firm, Ginger still hadn't met Larry, and meanwhile his wife had taken up with one of his friends. Elisa was constantly late to work, as was Sarah. It got to be so ridiculous that Ginger called Elisa up every morning to get her out of bed and let her boss know that she was in the office on time. Then, one day, Elisa took off with Sarah to go partying, apparently with Rick. "I was kind of irritated because I had been at work and was bored out of my mind and they were off partying," Ginger says.

By October, Elisa was lying to her own daughter

with stories of Sarah's "secret" boyfriend—the cover story used when Elisa and Sarah wanted to be alone together. "The only person that deeply knows Elisa is Sarah," Ginger said. "They're together and love each other like mother and daughter. They would lie to Haylei because Haylei would be jealous about the time they spent together."

She also saw Elisa get angry on the phone with Rick, and then saw her answer phones and lie about who she was to people on the receiving end— continuing a practice started before Larry died. "Every time someone would call, she'd fake and say she was me, Haylei, Sarah, or a fake person that she made up."

"Hello, is Elisa there?"

"No. Elisa isn't here right now. Can I take a message?" Elisa would say.

It could be comic at times, with Elisa disguising her voice.

But all of that paled in comparison to the temper tantrum Elisa threw when she realized the firm was losing far too much money. Without an actual lawyer present in the law firm, things weren't going so well. They also needed to renew Larry's license, and at first there didn't seem to be enough money in the firm's bank account to cover even that minor expense. Elisa went nuts. She threw office supplies off desks and began ripping things off the walls. Ginger watched in fear, cowed into silence as Elisa screamed and hit office furniture.

"We can't fucking practice! We're going to lose our fucking license and Larry's not here to fucking fix it!"

Elisa shouted one afternoon in the office as she tore the place asunder.

It was Sarah who calmed Elisa down and offered to find a lawyer they could farm work out to in order to keep the money flowing into the firm's accounts. Elisa then gathered her wits and sweet-talked a banker into helping her withdraw funds from an account to which Larry had sole access and put those funds into the business account where she could get at it. Her quick wits and good looks had served her well once more.

After taking a breath, things seemed to be okay again, briefly. The crisis had been averted. The proper license was paid for and to celebrate Sarah and Elisa took off again to party, leaving Ginger alone in the office. It was fine with Ginger at the time, whose opinion of them was changing. The only thing worse than Sarah and Elisa upset, she says, were Sarah and Elisa happy—and in the office. They were ugly, snotty people, she thought, who turned up their noses at those they perceived to be beneath them. "If you don't drive a nice car, Sarah is like, 'They're driving a rice rocket.' She says if you're going to drive a fucking Honda, then go to China or Japan," Ginger recalls.

Ginger also found them to be crass racists. According to a statement given to police, she said the two women trained Elisa's dog Morgan, or "Munchie," to dislike African Americans, and Sarah and Elisa constantly called them "niggers."

After several more days of partying, Ginger recalls Elisa and Sarah returning to the law office, and Elisa was once again in tears. Why? Because in her latest installment of *Where's Larry?*, the hapless yet intrepid attorney was trying to overcome his alcoholic tendencies, but now instead of a twenty-eight-day rehab, Larry had checked into a twelve-month rehab. Elisa wasn't sure it would work either, and that tore her apart because she loved Larry so much—or so she said to Ginger.

Meanwhile, Elisa volunteered that she hadn't had sex with Larry in several months and she told Ginger that it made her "skin crawl" when she touched him because he had loose skin and she wanted to touch someone with tight skin again. "However strange the case got, and that statement was certainly one of the strangest," an investigator said later, "we never actually thought Elisa was into necrophilia. It's just that knowing what we know afterward, that statement is pretty damn creepy." At the time she made the statements to Ginger, Larry was still packed away in the refrigerator in the garage of his own home.

Ginger didn't say much to Elisa about the stories Elisa told her about Larry and his whereabouts. Mostly she listened and noticed that Elisa "looked like crap" when she was talking with her and, on one occasion, was still wearing the same clothes she had on when she left the office three days ago.

Elisa was unraveling before Ginger's eyes. She had no way of knowing the care Elisa had taken with her appearance in the past, nor the elaborate plans she had put into place at a moment's notice to conceal and hide herself from friends and acquaintances. All Ginger knew was that her boss of a scant month was coming forth with details of a marriage, drinking, drugs, money, and other problems at the drop of a hat. Ginger also began to suspect that much of what was told to her was "bullshit." She was watching a show, a performance for her benefit, and while she found it creepily entertaining, at the same time it was increasingly frightening.

After she came back crying from her three-day party jag, Elisa also told Ginger that she was tired of Larry's alcoholic ways and that his kids "even hate him for it."

Meanwhile, Joe McNabney was happy to hear from Elisa, at least initially, that his father was in rehab again. Joe had seen him drink. "I thought, you know, great! Dad's getting what he needs."

Far from hating his father for his drinking, Joe expressed hope that his father was going to be all right again. The last time Larry checked into rehab, he came out ready to run marathons, so there was initially a good reason to feel hopeful. But Joe's happiness at hearing his father was in rehab eventually dwindled as Elisa changed the story, and as his father continued to be missing in action.

Ginger heard the stories Elisa told Joe and just shook her head. Her employer would sound sympathetic to Joe on the telephone and then, as soon as she hung up, would turn around and tell her what a horrible person he was. Elisa also cried to Ginger about Haylei's relationship with Larry. According to Elisa, he was constantly mean to Haylei. Joe McNabney and Haylei also said Larry wasn't too fond of Elisa's daughter, but the accusation brought a shrug from Ginger. She hadn't seen Haylei's mother treat her any better, after all. But she held her tongue.

Then Elisa said she was thinking of divorcing Larry because of the problems she was having with him. His drinking and his womanizing were just too much for her. She needed more stability in her life. She had already told a few other people that she was thinking of divorcing Larry, so it was no surprise to Ginger when Elisa told her the same thing. Then, a few days after being told that she was *thinking* about divorcing Larry, Elisa changed the story and began to tell everyone she had *already* divorced him. Ginger thought Elisa just got a good night's sleep and liked the sound of the last story so much that she began to use it whenever possible.

So, in the latest episode of *Where's Larry?* Larry and Elisa were divorced, but still friends, and naturally Elisa was still helping him out by running his law firm. Obviously, this was a good time for Elisa and Sarah to split for another three-day party, and they did. But for their latest sojourn into decadence and depravity, they had Ginger go down to the bank and cash checks made out to the McNabney law firm and bring several thousand dollars in cash back so they could buy new wardrobes. After all, the last time they went on a party spree, they came back wearing the same clothes they'd left in, and they just couldn't have that happen again.

It was no problem getting the checks made out to the firm converted into cash. Elisa signed Larry's name almost as well, if not better than he did before she killed him. Sarah and Haylei also got into the act of signing Larry's name on the checks. Haylei did it because her

In Memory of

Larry McNabney

Dec 19, 1948 ~ 2001

It's hard to understand why some
lives are taken before their time
Before they've lived their dreams,
Before their songs are sung...

But their lives go on forever
in the hearts and
lives they have touched...

Larry, you will remain in
the hearts of your friends forever!

Larry McNabney was a successful attorney and rising star on
the quarter horse circuit prior to his murder.

*Courtesy of Tavia McNabney Williams
and Joe McNabney*

Greg Whalen, Larry's mentor and horse trainer, was linked to Larry's wife, Elisa, through her efforts to hide Larry's murder.

Courtesy of the District Attorney, County of San Joaquin, CA

Larry in a photo from October 1973 with both of his daughters.

Courtesy of Tavia McNabney Williams and Joe McNabney

Larry in an early portrait about the time he and Ron Bath became partners.

Courtesy of Tavia McNabney Williams and Joe McNabney

Larry, shaving with his young son.

Courtesy of Tavia McNabney Williams and Joe McNabney

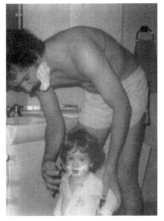

Larry ran a marathon shortly after leaving rehab.

Courtesy of Tavia McNabney Williams and Joe McNabney

Ginger Miller, the young secretary hired by the McNabney law firm, became suspicious when she was never able to meet Larry McNabney. Police credit her tip for opening the case against Sarah Dutra and Elisa McNabney.

Courtesy of Ginger Miller

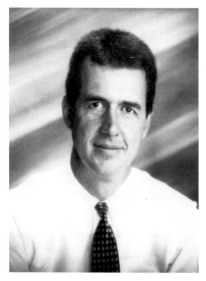

Tom Hogan, Laren Sims's family friend and attorney.

Courtesy of Tom Hogan

Sarah Dutra's booking photo.
*Courtesy of the District Attorney,
County of San Joaquin, CA*

Laren Sims's booking photo.
*Courtesy of the Hernando
County Sheriff's Dept.*

Larry with his stepdaughter Tavia Williams.

*Courtesy of
Tavia McNabney Williams
and Joe McNabney*

Larry at the wedding
of Tavia Williams.

*Courtesy of
Tavia McNabney Williams
and Joe McNabney*

One of Larry's last portraits.

*Courtesy of Tavia McNabney Williams
and Joe McNabney*

Mountain View Cemetery, Reno, Nevada

*Courtesy of Tavia McNabney Williams
and Joe McNabney*

Larry with his beloved horse Ima Town Celebrity.

*Courtesy of Tavia McNabney Williams
and Joe McNabney*

mother told her to, and Sarah did it because she wanted to.

Sarah became so interested in and dedicated to the art of forgery that she began to practice signing Larry's name on steno and legal pads. When Ginger saw this, Sarah explained she had to be ready to sign checks because "sometimes Elisa is gone and she has to pay us or the bills." She never offered a sound explanation as to why Larry couldn't sign them, but by then Ginger had gotten used to the subterfuge. She hardly even blinked when Sarah told her that the best way to get rid of the evidence of the forgery was to burn the paper on which she had practiced Larry's signature. However, Ginger did get concerned when she saw Haylei, while practicing Larry's signature, nearly set the carpet in the office on fire trying to hide the evidence.

The strange events at the McNabney law firm made Ginger determined to keep a low profile, but even as she tried, she raised the ire of one of her new bosses—Sarah. She and Ginger soon found themselves at odds, ironically, over the pet dog that allegedly cost Larry his life.

Ginger didn't like being recruited as a chauffeur and pet sitter for Munchie, Elisa's dog. Elisa would put the dog in a kennel for weeks at a time. A Jack Russell terrier that was inherently hyperactive to begin with, he became more so when caged in the kennel or locked up in the law office—and Elisa did both constantly. She tried to counter the problem by giving the dog Prozac. This didn't endear Elisa to Ginger, but what Sarah did with her dog Ralphie made Ginger angry in the extreme.

Ralphie was the dog that Sarah cared so much for that the night she was busy killing Larry she had to leave to take care of him. She was so mindful of the dog's needs that she decided, since Ginger had taken Elisa's dog to the kennel, Ginger could take Ralphie to her parents' home in Vacaville, California. It was enough that Ginger had to pamper Elisa, who was the employer; she didn't feel like she had to pamper Sarah, who supposedly was another secretary like herself.

The working conditions deteriorated even more for Ginger in the middle of October when a company from the Los Angeles area called up and not only wanted money, but wanted their wheelchair back too. Ginger had no idea what the problem was, but again she saw Elisa go into a snit. Ginger knew that money was tight at the firm, and her first thought was that is why Elisa freaked out. She had no idea of the history behind the wheelchair.

So, life went on at the McNabney law firm, *sans* Larry, as the blustery month of October ended. By the first part of November a new wind had blown into town and Ginger was hearing complaints about Larry from everyone in the office. Sarah hated him. Elisa hated him, and she said even his own children hated him.

As for Haylei's relationship with Larry, it hadn't been the best either. Ken Redelsperger liked Haylei and had a much better relationship with her. Where Ken had gone horseback riding with her and Elisa, or taught Haylei to ride Motocross, Larry had extended a cold shoulder. Where Ken included her in most of his planning with Elisa, and even kept Haylei in his home when Larry and Elisa had taken trips alone, Larry shoed Haylei away.

Naturally, Haylei's relationship with Larry was strained. She saw him as mean and thought Larry took her away from her mother. She hated him because of that, or so she had said. Part of it was definitely Larry's fault. He was not fond of Haylei and had voiced his own concerns about her, mostly by describing her as a "spoiled little bitch."

But some thought that Elisa cultivated this caustic relationship. Her motivation, as the reasoning goes, was selfish. Though Haylei put a crimp in her partying lifestyle, Elisa loved her daughter and usually liked her being around. And if Larry got upset with and ultimately pushed Haylei away, it enabled Elisa to play good cop to Larry's bad cop.

Ginger, for one, thought that Haylei had been misled. She believed Elisa didn't want Haylei around and used Larry as cover. As for Haylei herself, Ginger found her to be a brat and a blabbermouth. When Elisa had a conflict with Haylei, Ginger watched her toss money at the girl to make her shut up or go away. Ginger found it an interesting mother-daughter dynamic. She thought they were more like friends or sisters who couldn't always get along than mother and daughter.

As for Haylei's relationship with Sarah, Ginger thought Sarah was "ruthless."

But then, Sarah was ruthless with most people in her life, not just Haylei, and what Ginger saw made her believe there wasn't much Sarah wouldn't do—if it was for her own benefit.

"She likes to be with married men or men that have girlfriends," Ginger said. "She just wants to have sex with them because she's going to marry rich and she'll have a rich older man for her husband later on."

In short, Sarah was the embodiment of the worst fear of every single man in his mid-life. In the search for a trophy wife, men often forget there are heavy strings attached. With Sarah it was more like a rope. "She's a home wrecker, or a character in an Eagles' song," one of the police investigators said.

Sarah's contempt for other people reached outside of the McNabney office. Those who saw her at college during the time when she and Elisa were conspiring to hide Larry's body and conceal the murder said she was distant and aloof. One day at school, a fellow student who had noticed Sarah driving a red BMW said, "Gosh that's a really nice car for a student."

"Thanks, I worked really hard for it," Sarah replied.

Back at the law firm, Ginger couldn't help but notice that despite all of the activity in the office, there was still no Larry around. There was plenty of talk about him, but the man who owned the firm was conspicuous in his absence, especially when three different women forged his name on every check deposited. The rats were not only taking over the ship, but eating it.

Ginger's concern for the firm's owner soon graduated to outright worry. She already suspected the Addams Family would make better bosses than Elisa and Sarah, but now, though she'd never met him—never even set eyes on him—she feared for Larry's safety. Nothing seemed to make sense. She was working in a bizarre environment that wasn't getting any better.

At the time, Sarah and Elisa were still living inside the McNabney home, while Larry continued to reside in the refrigerator. And they still went to horse shows and sold off or gave away Larry's worldly possessions. Haylei and Ginger lived on the fringes of this dark whirlwind and were deceived by the constant motion, if by nothing else. Every aspect of Sarah's and Elisa's lives became a giant shell game. Only there was no pearl under the shell. Just Larry, and he was still dead.

As the weeks passed, Sarah and Elisa, already deemed inseparable from each other by those closest to them, became even more so. Without each other, Ginger said, there would have been no social life for the two women. "They're snobs and no one wants to be their friends," she explained.

Apparently, few wanted to have anything to do with them at work either. The office was only populated by Sara, Elisa, Ginger, and Haylei, and by the end of October the firm was in serious financial trouble, despite Elisa telling Haylei and others that they could run the business perfectly without an attorney. Soon, she had to bring in an outside attorney to keep the cash spigots turned on. The wolves were beginning to circle as they got all kinds of calls from bill collectors demanding money. The landlord was even threatening eviction. It was an ugly situation.

Making a surprise visit to the offices one day, the landlord spotted a bit of marijuana on the desk. When queried, Elisa didn't try to hide the fact that it was indeed the evil weed, she just quickly apologized for it, said it must belong to an employee, and promised to fire the offending employee immediately.

But the dope did belong to her, and at the end of October, when the landlord finally decided to kick her out of the office, she blew out of the office taking her dope with her.

Prior to the inevitable eviction, there was also another horse show Elisa had to visit, and before that she brought Ginger the latest installment of *Where's Larry?*

In this episode of the exciting adventure, Larry decided to chuck his worldly cares and join a cult with guys he'd known all of his life. He was happy in his new cult environment and was so blissful that he probably would never return.

Ginger shook her head.

Elisa seemed briefly happy at that point, but that ended abruptly a few days later when she struggled with Haylei and they ended up throwing things at each other. No one could seem to remember why.

Office life then eventually settled back to what was considered normal in the McNabney firm after each explosive incident played itself out. For Ginger, each day working there seemed more like something culled from television shows than reality.

When Elisa went to the horse show that month, she left Sarah and Haylei behind, and Sarah decided it was time to treat Ginger to her own television show staring Larry. In her edition of *Where's Larry?* she had just talked to Larry on the telephone and he was at the horse show with Elisa, having a grand old time.

By then Ginger was tired and not particularly interested in a job *and* a show anymore. Fed up with all of the lies, all she wanted was to get a paycheck. But by November, just six weeks into working for Elisa and Sarah, she was told that the firm was running out of money and she couldn't be paid. Then things got interesting. Ginger went for a week and a half without a paycheck while her bills piled up. Her anger and displeasure with Elisa and Sarah escalated as she watched the two women continue to "live large." She noticed that they certainly weren't short of cash. So she called Haylei, looking for Elisa, who was still out on the road.

Haylei said she didn't know where her mother was but she would try to call her. When Haylei didn't call her back, Ginger called again and left a message stressing that she had been unable to get hold of Elisa for a week and she needed a paycheck. It seemed like only moments later that she got a call from a very irate and agitated Elisa, who was offering her a variety of threats.

"Look, you fucking bitch," Elisa shouted. "I want you to fucking know. Don't you ever call my fucking daughter again and ever fucking talk to her about money again, because if you do, I'm going to kick your little fucking ass, you stupid bitch!"

Ginger was taken aback. She'd never seen the infamous Florida temper flare up this high, even when Elisa fought with her daughter. Ginger wasn't sure where the anger came from. All she knew was that she needed to get paid and, as she said later, that "no one has ever spoken to me like that in my entire life."

But whatever else was going to happen, Ginger was determined not to back down. She told Elisa that she didn't have to give her the paycheck if she didn't want to, but that she could go to the police and talk about some of the more interesting forgery activities going on at the McNabney law firm.

This had the effect of a cattle prod on Elisa. She was still living with a stiff in the refrigerator, after all, and had no desire for police to come calling.

"You fucking bitch! You mind your own business," Elisa shouted back. "I'll talk to you when I get back, and you know what, I'm going to listen to my fucking daughter's machine and if I think you're being rude, you're out. I'm going to fuck you up!"

After doing her Scarface impersonation, Elisa hung up. Five minutes later, according to Ginger, Sarah called her playing good cop. She was conciliatory and offered a loan to Ginger, who said that it was okay, she could borrow twenty dollars from her aunt to hold her over—she just wanted her paycheck.

A few days later Elisa returned and apologized for her behavior, but Ginger had reached the point of no return. "From that moment on, I never had a friendship with anybody in that office," she says. It was all strictly business. She wanted her money, and Elisa put her off as Ginger had seen Elisa do to every other person to whom she was in debt.

The problems at the firm troubled Ginger, who did not initially have bad feelings toward Sarah or Elisa. She *wanted* to like them. "I was so deeply mad inside because I did love them at first," she says of Elisa. "I considered them my friends. I couldn't believe that she would talk to me that way."

Elisa tried several excuses for her behavior on the phone and for not returning Ginger's telephone call.

"Her cell phone was broken," Ginger recalls her saying. "She was busy, and she had been up all night talking to Larry because they had so many things to talk about when Elisa got to the horse show."

Again, Sarah offered to loan her money. But Ginger was in no mood and countered with an ominous threat of her own, telling Sarah, "A hungry mouth talks . . ."

While Sarah and Elisa tried to decide what to do with Ginger's veiled threat, something else occurred during mid-November that got them jumping. Cheryl Jensen, the landlord for the Woodbridge home, came by the home to adjust the property's sprinklers. The sprinkler controls, it happened, were just behind the refrigerator in the garage.

As she casually tweaked the controls, Cheryl Jensen asked Elisa where Larry was. He was less than a foot away, inside the refrigerator, but as calmly as she could, Elisa told Cheryl he was away visiting family. Cheryl smiled, finished adjusting the sprinklers, and left shortly afterward.

Cheryl never knew how close she was to discovering the truth.

On the other hand, Ginger thought she was getting closer to a truth she didn't want to know. All of the lies, the games, and the arguments over pay had convinced her that she might be in danger herself from Elisa and Sarah, who certainly didn't need a mouthy secretary running around telling police about malfeasance and forgery at the McNabney law firm.

Ginger came to fear so much for her life that she began leaving notes for relatives about where she was and what she was doing, in case she ever turned up missing. "When I was still working there after that time, if she had me go anywhere," Ginger later told police, "I would leave the time that I left and where I was going and tell my family because she could have me knocked off somewhere."

She was stressed out. She'd had to deal with an increasingly strange atmosphere in a work environment she felt was caustic and eventually came to see as an ongoing criminal enterprise. She wasn't paid in a timely fashion, had been threatened, and began to believe those threats.

So, at the end of November, after working, nominally for Larry McNabney for about ten weeks, Ginger made the move that broke the case open: She called the police and reported Larry, the boss she never met, missing. It was November 30, 2001. Larry had been dead more than two and a half months and was still in the refrigerator of his own home.

At first the police didn't know what to think when he was reported missing, and neither did the press. At the time, there were complaints from clients, landlords, bill collectors, and scores of others who claimed Larry McNabney owed them money. His disappearance could've been engineered so he could escape with his clients' money and leave the country, to be followed later by his trophy wife. Indeed, there was little evidence to suspect foul play. There was little evidence to suspect anything other than a lawyer on the run.

Only Ginger had an independent, inside track as to what was really going on in the law firm. If Larry were on the run, why had she *never* heard from him? Ginger thought she at least should have encountered him in some form or fashion once or twice, perhaps answering a phone, or answering a door. But, to her, there was never any doubt that Larry just hadn't been around—at least since she'd been hired.

In the beginning, with little to go on, investigators looked at the possibility of Larry being on the run as one of many scenarios as December 2001 rolled around.

12

So What's in the Trunk?

Living each day with Larry in the refrigerator was taking its toll on Sarah and Elisa as they plodded through work, systematically tearing apart, selling, and giving away everything Larry had ever built in his life.

Their vampirelike activities extended to sucking the life out of not only Larry, but his business and his reputation, which plummeted in the months after his disappearance and before his body was discovered.

If it had been up to Sarah and Elisa, though, the body would never have been discovered. They finally decided they had a plan to get rid of it. Larry always loved Las Vegas, and Elisa decided it would be a good idea to show respect for him by putting him in an unmarked hole somewhere in the hardscrabble desert near the gambling mecca of the world.

Hunter Thompson found something venal, vile, and yet hauntingly attractive in the madness of Las Vegas.

It was a favorite stomping ground for Larry, and Elisa and Sarah loved it too.

During previous visits to Sin City, Elisa and Sarah, dressed for sexual excess, would walk into bars like women out of a Robert Palmer music video, smiling and strutting and turning heads everywhere they went.

"They were total mind fuckers," one police officer working the case said of the two.

But more important, they were also murderers with Larry's body to dispose of, and in November they still were having a difficult time doing it. Before the end of that month, when Ginger Miller called in a missing persons report on a boss she had never met, Elisa and Sarah had taken a trip to Las Vegas for fun in the sun and to find a dignified place to bury Larry in the shade.

It was another road trip in the movie running in Elisa's head. It was "Thelma and Louise Part Deux," starring Elisa McNabney and Sarah Dutra as they packed up and headed east on Interstate 15 in the little Jaguar Elisa had leased. Together they took Larry out of the refrigerator—cold, lifeless, and looking very fresh from his extended stay in temperatures just above freezing—and managed to stuff him in the trunk of the car. Elisa took great pains, later while in police custody, to describe the effort it took for her and Sarah to get Larry into the trunk. It involved a spare tire and a lot of luck.

"I was stunned when she told us how she did it," a police officer said. "They were inventive."

Larry was just too large for Elisa to handle alone, so

once again she employed the help of her willing assistant Sarah. Using a spare trailer tire from their horse trailer, they opened up the refrigerator where Larry was resting. Putting the tire flat on the floor next to the refrigerator, they nudged Larry out and he rolled quietly into the tire. Then the two women pushed him and the tire from the refrigerator to the Jaguar, parked inside the garage.

The size of the tire was large enough, and the silhouette of the Jaguar so low, that there was very little height differential between the tire and the open trunk. The two women merely pushed him into the open trunk, slammed down the lid, got their two favorite dogs, tossed them in the car, gathered up as much marijuana as they could scrounge, and left home.

They were off to Vegas. Naturally, it was a trauma to be driving with a dead body in the trunk, so the two women smoked marijuana like cigarette chain smokers from the moment they left California.

Stoned to the gills, giggling like schoolgirls and playing with their puppies, they finally arrived at the Bellagio Hotel in Vegas. A beautiful, large, modern hotel owned by Andy Garcia in the remake of *Ocean's Eleven*, it was the perfect scene for the two women to have fun.

As they pulled into the hotel a bellman approached them. "May I get your luggage?" he asked.

Sarah, who was driving, as always, nodded. She didn't even give it a thought, or perhaps more accurately, because of her marijuana intake, she had forgotten completely about Larry, who was residing in the trunk. So she hit the button to pop the trunk.

At the same time, Elisa, who was stoned but had the survival instincts of a shark, was horrorstruck by the thought of a stranger popping the trunk to find her cold, dead husband wrapped in plastic like a leftover dinner, so even as Sarah waved the bellman on, Elisa hopped out of the passenger side of the convertible and made it to the trunk in time to slam the lid down before the startled bellman could see what was inside.

"No, that's okay," Elisa, said. "We'll get it."

With that said and done, they quickly changed their mind about staying at the Bellagio, hopped back into the car and drove down the road to another hotel nearby.

Their little dramatic scene at the Bellagio served to remind them of the primary reason for making the trip to Vegas. They had to bury Larry. Elisa, after all, wanted a proper burial for her husband, in a hole near the town and the famous Strip he loved so much. But again it didn't work out the way she wanted.

During their trip to Vegas, the women had decided to buy a shovel at a Home Depot. They had already purchased a couple of shovels the first time they tried to bury Larry, but after he died and they stuffed him in the refrigerator, Elisa said they had thrown away those two shovels. "We got sick every time we'd go into the garage, so we threw them in the Dumpster," she told police. So, by the time the women decided to bury Larry in Vegas, they needed a shovel.

And why did she get sick every time she went into her garage? the police wanted to know. "Because I knew my husband was dead and in the refrigerator and I put him there, you know, and I'm like, 'Oh my God, I can't believe I did this.' "

Sarah and the dogs stayed in the hotel while Elisa drove outside of town, looking for an appropriate place to bury Larry. It was a Friday night, and Elisa said she drove around but couldn't find a proper resting place. The following night, after a hard day in the casinos, Elisa was back at it and finally found a spot that wasn't too remote and that was apparently adequate for her needs. She was thankful for all of two minutes, right up until the time she began to dig the hole.

The hard-baked desert pan was so difficult to dig up that she could barely scratch the surface. So she drove back to the hotel in a panic and after giving the Jaguar over to valet parking, ran inside the hotel to cry to Sarah about the latest fiasco. "I told her I can't do it, and the whole time he's in the trunk, you know, and we're in valet parking and it's not good, you know," Elisa later said.

Luckily for both women, the valet attendants never popped open the trunk. A few minutes later, the women decided to give up and blew out of town with Larry still residing in the trunk and Elisa suffering from heat exhaustion.

As it turned out, Tavia Williams said there was even a cinematic tie-in to Elisa's desire to bury Larry near a place he loved. "She saw it in a movie," Tavia explained. Elisa had apparently seen a feature film in which a woman killed her husband, buried him in the desert outside of Las Vegas, and got away with the murder for a very long time. Elisa didn't have the same luck, so with Sarah and the dogs along for the ride, and Larry in the back, they eagerly returned to their home outside of Sacramento.

But by then Sarah was tired of having Larry in the refrigerator. She wanted him gone, and told Elisa she would have to do it herself because she planned to leave town for a while.

Truth be told, though, getting rid of the body was almost an afterthought to them. By the middle of November, Larry had been dead for more than two months and no one had come around looking for him. The few people who had were easy enough to deflect. If only they could make some more money, it seemed no one would ever bother to find out what happened to Larry.

Erik Roen, the owner of the White Diamonds Ranch, ran across both women in mid-November at the World Show in Oklahoma City, and he said neither one seemed to have a care in the world. He told police they were in "racing form" and "out to party."

His encounter began with Elisa, a woman he barely knew, as he sat to watch the horse show. She sidled up to him and sat down. She smelled good and looked better, and she was interested in talking. Erik was a married man, so whatever she had to say wasn't going to go too far, but a man can listen, and Elisa liked to talk. She told him she was unhappy in her relationship with Larry and had been for a while. Couldn't anyone understand she was just a party girl out looking for a good time and Larry wasn't it?

Erik smiled and didn't say much, and a few minutes later Sarah walked up and sat near them. Elisa was talking about how she wanted to buy some land in Texas, but Erik's attention turned to Sarah, who wanted to know what he and Elisa were talking about.

"We were talking about you," Elisa cooed.

At that point Erik sensed the sexual tension that could end up with all three of them naked in a bed somewhere, and because he didn't want to go down that road, he excused himself. "I have to get ready to show," he said politely, and left the two to their own company.

Later that evening he was getting ready to leave the practice arena to celebrate his son's birthday when he got a call on his cell phone. His sister and the rest of the people in his group were already at their hotel, waiting to go out for the birthday celebration. Could he catch a ride to them, rather than someone coming to pick him up?

At that moment, Elisa caught his eye, as she sat in her red Jaguar not thirty feet away. He wasn't interested in a sexual liaison with her, but perhaps she might give him a ride to his family.

"Are you going back to the hotel?" he asked her.

"Sure," she said.

"Can I catch a ride with you?"

She was more than willing to oblige, so Erik told his sister he got a ride and was on his way. Then he got in the car, and a few seconds later, as they were pulling away, Sarah ran up and jumped into the backseat of the Jaguar. Elisa smiled and pulled out a marijuana pipe. Erik was startled, since he didn't smoke, but even more startled when Sarah quickly leaned across his lap as she reached for the glove box in the front seat, opened it and produced a big bag of pot. Erik was uncomfortable, not only with the pot, but with the beautiful woman draped across his lap.

"You do smoke. Everybody parties," Elisa purred as she caught his look of discomfort.

"No. Just give me whiskey," Erik replied.

He almost got out of the car then, as Elisa and Sarah openly passed the pipe between them while Elisa drove to the hotel. But Erik decided he could suffer the company of two reasonably attractive women smoking dope for a few minutes for the sake of a ride to his son's party.

When they got to the hotel a few minutes later, Elisa asked Erik if he wanted to go and party with her and Sarah. For some men it would have been a toss-up. Do you take the two bimbos in a threesome, or do you go home for your son's birthday party? He excused himself, said he had to go see his son, and left.

When he got up the next morning, he could see the aftermath of the hell Sarah and Elisa had set in motion after he turned down their offer. Erik ran into Elisa in the hallway of the hotel. She looked "pretty messed up," he said.

Wearing a low-cut, hip-hugging pair of Levi's jeans and a cutoff T-shirt that prominently displayed the bottoms of her large breasts, Elisa looked like anything but the classy woman she often pretended to be. She was also so stoned and drunk she didn't know where her own car was, and asked Erik for help finding it. As it turned out, it wasn't too hard to find, since it was still in the parking lot of the hotel.

After that chance encounter, over the next few weeks when Elisa returned home, she tried several times to get Erik to come over to her place and party with her, but he never did. At one point she said she was ordering a truck and wanted his advice on it, if he could drive up to her place. He replied that she could come over to his house if she was interested and they could talk about it there. She made the appointment but never showed up.

Time and again, stories of Elisa and Sarah's partying and sexual escapades made the rounds of the quarter horse circuit. Had anyone known about the dead man, it would have seemed that they could, and would, get away with anything. But there was just one little problem: Ginger Miller. She had gone through some of the law firm's paperwork and been witness to some shady bank transactions. Without Elisa's knowledge, Ginger had also been gathering information about credit cards that were used but didn't have Elisa's name on them. She was also beginning to confront Elisa on some of her lies and that had Elisa worried.

One day, Elisa sent Ginger to a chiropractor's office in her BMW to pick up some paperwork and told her to tell anyone who might ask that Ginger was driving Larry's car. Ginger balked. "If I tell them that's Larry's car, how do I know that's not just an alibi to say Larry is around?" Ginger later told reporters.

By December, Elisa was ready with a new production of *Where's Larry?* In her latest installment, Larry was back in town but was loving life on a golfing trip and wouldn't be around too much. By then Ginger wasn't having any of Elisa's nonsense and had gone to the police. She even noted on a trip to the McNabney home that Larry's golf clubs were still hanging on a hook in the garage, apparently unused and, to her eyes, seemingly hadn't been used in a while.

Ginger also noticed very little evidence that a man had been in the house at all. It wasn't just that all the toilet seats were always down, but there were no men's clothes anywhere. The shoes stacked by the door all belonged to women, as did every piece of clothing she'd seen going to and coming from the cleaners. "She told me he was living there," Ginger later said. "She told me that she really wanted me to meet Larry and they were supposed to go to coffee together. She wanted me to meet Larry so bad. But he was always gone. She would also say that I just missed him by ten minutes." What Ginger didn't and couldn't know was that Larry actually was in the house every time she visited—still refrigerated in the garage.

But Ginger did know two very important things: She hadn't met Larry, and by December, Elisa still owed her money. After calling the cops, she knew it might take a while to get some action, and in the meantime she still had to work for Elisa, knowing full well that if she left, she'd never get the money Elisa owed her. It was difficult for her, and increasingly so when she saw Elisa lying to Larry's son Joe. That worried her immensely. On several occasions when Joe called, Elisa answered the phone and told him different lies than she had just told Ginger about Larry—and while Ginger was in the office.

Ginger told her family she thought something was seriously wrong with Larry. "I've never heard his voice," she said, and also told them that she thought Elisa hated her husband because "every time she talked about him she had rage."

Ironically, it was Ginger who cared more for Larry, a

man she'd never met, than either his own wife or secretary did. Their behavior sickened Ginger, and after she called the police, her suspicions were aroused once again when Elisa and Sarah began to turn on the charm for her. But by then it could not influence her. "The only reason she was pulling me in so close is because she does want to watch me and make sure I don't talk," Ginger said. "That's the only reason she started pulling me in closer, to make her enemy her friend. That's the best thing you can do, and I knew she was doing that."

It was now a cat and mouse game for Ginger at the firm, and she tried to stay away from the bait Elisa offered. So, when Elisa invited her to spend Christmas dinner with her and Larry, Ginger didn't have to hear that Larry backed out at the last second. She had already decided she wasn't going to go to dinner with Elisa and Sarah. "She was mad that I didn't go. I didn't trust what would happen," Ginger says. After Christmas, Elisa invited her to party at a ranch where she said they were going to pick up some cute-looking cowboys, but again Ginger turned her down. "The last thing I wanted to do was be in the middle of nowhere with her and Sarah," she told police.

By then Ginger was often working out of Elisa's house, since they had been evicted from the office. Elisa told Ginger they were moving into another office with an attorney who had cancer and who Larry wanted to buy out. But, then again, Elisa said Larry was burned out and didn't want to go back into the office, that he had been in rehab, or golfing, or traveling, or many other things. In her latest installment of *Where's Larry?* she had Larry living back at home with her, ready to resume their life together, even though they were supposedly divorced. Wouldn't you know it; Ginger just kept missing Larry by five minutes too. A few weeks before she'd missed him by ten minutes, so it seemed that progress was being made. But there was still no Larry.

If he were around, Ginger wondered what he'd think of the furniture and worldly possessions being sold or given away at a record pace by his wife. After one of the beds was sold, Ginger had to wonder where everyone was sleeping. If Larry were actually still around, he would have had to share his bed with Elisa, Sarah, and Haylei. Later Haylei said it was just three women—Sarah, her mother, and her—all sharing the same bed.

"It was like a giant slap in the face to Larry, for Sarah and Elisa to be sleeping in his bed and he was dead in the garage," detective Deborah Scheffel later said.

There were other, far colder slaps in Larry's face. Elisa had begun wearing his Rolex even before the body was cold. She also took his favorite horseshoe-shaped ring with diamonds in it and wore it on a chain around her neck. Then she took the ring to a jeweler and wanted the diamonds removed and set in a pendant for her. Another slap.

In December 2001 and on into the New Year, Ginger had a hard time going to work. Suspicious, and upset at the amount of money she saw Sarah and Elisa waste, she now also wondered how far the two of them would go.

Elisa was so extravagant in her spending that after

having her hair styled, she once tipped the hairdresser $150, and then another $150 on top of that. All of this while Ginger was still having trouble getting her paycheck. The women were hanging bad paper so often that people were beginning to refuse any check written by the McNabney law firm.

Any credibility Larry had was spent along with all of his money after he died. "They robbed the man of everything," prosecutor Tom Testa says. "They took his house, his cars, his money, his reputation, and his life. They stopped at nothing." Elisa meanwhile was giving Ginger stacks of clothes to take to the cleaners, along with wads of cash with instructions to have the clothes cleaned in an hour or two. Then Elisa wouldn't pick up the clothes for three or four days. "They were always wasting money like that," Ginger says.

By early December the physical effects of the heavy partying, the tension of living in a house with a dead body, and the subterfuge it took to keep everything going were showing on Elisa and Sarah. With their massive intake of diet pills, the two had effectively stopped eating, dropping several dress sizes and a lot of weight, despite their prodigious use of marijuana, which usually induces a bad case of the "munchies." Sarah claimed to have lost sixty-five pounds, and Elisa lost a smaller but still significant amount.

Witnesses say the two began to resemble living scarecrows, with sunken eyes and pinched cheeks. Others said they began to look like the vampires they had become.

Finally, after returning from Vegas, and just before Larry's fifty-third birthday, Elisa could take it no more. She got rid of Larry's body. She claimed she did it by herself, a spurious claim that prosecutors never believed.

It was a rainy, muddy night when she drove to a vineyard not more than fifteen miles from where she and Larry had lived together. She claimed she was able to turn up the ground and dig a hole that was at least thigh deep. Then she pulled and pushed the body into the muddy pit. From there she tried to remove clothes and plastic, anything that could be identified or hold DNA or other physical evidence and could be traced back to her. Elisa said Sarah instructed her to do all of that, including cutting everything she could off Larry with a pair of scissors. She then buried him in the ground, took the articles of clothing and drove all over Sacramento to different Dumpsters, disposing of all the evidence.

Prosecutor Testa and the police who investigated the case came to believe that Elisa had help in disposing of Larry's body, perhaps that of an undocumented worker who labored in the area on a ranch, but they were never able to prove it.

They never believed that Greg Whalen assisted her in removing the body, even though his workers later came and carted away the refrigerator that had been Larry's final resting place for so many months. Greg, after all, was a close friend and admired Larry. Prosecutors did not believe, even later when some questioned his character, that he could have had anything to do with throwing Larry in a shallow ditch.

No one had a hard time believing that Elisa, in her callous and cold-blooded mode, would have a problem with it, though. She later said as much when she claimed she buried her husband alone. She picked the vineyard, she said, because Larry loved his Chardonnay and she wanted him to rest comfortably near his beloved grapes.

The day after she buried him, she drove back out to the area, and when she saw some cars there, panicked, thinking the body had already been found. She didn't know there was housing for migrant workers within a mile of where she had buried her husband. When she figured it out, she still didn't rest well. She told Sarah she thought she had buried the body in a grave that was too shallow. On several occasions she would drive by the location to see if anything had been found.

A few times she even had her daughter with her. "Let's go for a ride," she said.

Inevitably, they would always take the same trip, traveling down the same road near the same vineyard. Haylei wondered about that. Not until the night before Elisa was captured did Haylei learn why they always took that route.

13

The Bitch Is Following Me Again

Ginger Miller had perhaps the greatest insight into what was going on in the McNabney law firm and household after Sarah and Elisa killed Larry. Her weeks inside the meat grinder of the firm helped police in ways they couldn't even fathom as the case began to break. But she wasn't alone in going to the police. Joe McNabney and a woman from the Bronx named Joyce Blair Carter also helped immensely.

Joyce hired Larry shortly before his death after her husband was injured in a car accident. After mediation, Joyce had high hopes of getting enough money to take care of her husband, the car, and some very large doctor's expenses. But, it wasn't to be that way.

Joyce began calling the firm in November and continued to call into December, looking for about $150,000 in settlement checks Larry was supposed to get to her. Elisa had taken the checks and cashed them, but hadn't forwarded the money to Joyce. Another client, Alfred Torres, began showing up looking for his money, and Elisa was avoiding him too.

Joyce, however, wouldn't go away. Ginger knew that Elisa had cashed checks for Joyce that the insurance company had delivered, but didn't know that Elisa hadn't passed the money on. When Joyce continued to call, sounding desperate and crying, Ginger realized what had happened and got upset. She apologized for Elisa and told Joyce what she knew.

Elisa nearly met her match in a very angry Joyce Blair Carter. Joyce said she spoke to Elisa on September 11, while Elisa was busy with Sarah murdering Larry. The call angered Elisa, and she abruptly hung up on Joyce after telling her she was busy with something.

After Ginger told Joyce what had happened with her money, Joyce became a gadfly in Elisa's life. "I stalked her," Joyce said bluntly. "I'd call her twenty times a day. I checked into all of her financial holdings and I kept after her. I wanted my money."

This produced some interesting results as Joyce watched Elisa dangle at the end of a string of her own making. Once, Elisa left a message on Joyce's answering machine saying she had lost her own cell phone and couldn't get in touch with her. Another time she left a message saying, "We'll have to let Larry handle it." The lies she told Joyce were thinly veiled but expertly delivered. Joyce still has two of them on her answering machine. Elisa betrayed little emotion as she spun her Machiavellian web of deceit. She could have been ordering off a take-out menu as she described Larry being ready to intercede and handle the case, even though he had been dead nearly two months at the time.

Otherwise, Elisa would see Joyce coming and simply avoid her. On at least one occasion before Elisa was evicted from Larry's offices, she pulled into the parking lot in her car only to see Joyce in her car watching her. Elisa quickly parked, popped open the door to the Jaguar, and bolted for the safe confines of her office, where she quickly closed and locked the door.

When she got inside she said, "That bitch is following me again." It was almost comical.

Joyce didn't know what was going on, but she didn't care. She wanted her money, and she got tired of Elisa's obvious lies. "She's one sick bitch," Joyce said.

Another day, Joyce followed Elisa in her car to a hotel. She had notions of ramming Elisa's car with her own. With one eye on Elisa, Joyce called her husband on his cell phone with her own and confessed her diabolical plan. "Don't do it," he told her, and after a few minutes of his entreaties, Joyce backed down. But she seethed over being manipulated by Elisa and Sarah. Naturally, Joyce wanted to speak to Larry. After all, Larry was the attorney. But Elisa had begun dealing out a healthy dose of lies to Joyce about Larry's whereabouts, confusing matters. But, Joyce wasn't buying any of it. "I said, who do you think you're talking to?" Joyce said to Elisa one day. "Nothing you say makes sense. You're not even a good liar. I'm from the Bronx."

Her deep Bronx sensitivities drove her to become

her own investigator, supplying information to the police when she got it, bugging them to move faster on the case against Elisa, and alternately pumping Ginger for information while supplying moral support to her for staying in the firm. In some regards, she became Ginger's lifeline, talking to the secretary at least once a day and helping her stay focused as things progressed. "She is a remarkable young woman," Joyce says of Ginger. "Here was a girl who was about the same age as Sarah. She got the job to help her through college, and she could've gone the way Sarah went, but she went in the exact opposite direction."

The more she got into the case, the more Joyce became convinced that something had happened to Larry. Finally, in the first few weeks of January, just days before Elisa fled for good, Joyce called her up and said, "I think you killed your husband." Elisa didn't offer much in denial, but she didn't have to, and Joyce wouldn't have cared or believed her if she had.

Before many gave up hope of finding Larry alive, Joyce knew what had gone on. After all, she was raised in the Bronx.

Joe McNabney, on the other hand, held out hope for far longer than most did, and while he wasn't raised in the Bronx, he did begin to get the feeling something wasn't right about life in the law firm and in his father's house after September 11, 2001. In November, Sarah called Joe—"in a little happy voice," he said—trying to make nice with him for reasons he couldn't fathom.

"Hey, Joe, you want to come out and party with Elisa and me?" Sarah asked him.

"Where's my dad?" Joe responded.

"Out of town," Sarah coyly purred back. Of course, he was sitting in the refrigerator downstairs while Sarah was inviting the murdered man's son out to party next to his father's corpse. "Bram Stoker should have such an imagination," Joyce Blair Carter said when she heard of the invitation.

"I'll call you back in five minutes," Joe said. Then he hung up and called his mother Jodee, Larry's second wife.

"Don't you dare go out there," she said. It wasn't that she thought the two women would kill him, but a sexual threesome definitely seemed a possibility, and even Joe thought Elisa had, in the past, expressed more than a matronly interest in him. But the bottom line for Joe was that he thought his dad would get angry with him for being out there without him, and there was always the possibility that Elisa could lie about what happened while he was there. "I didn't want to piss my dad off," he said. So he didn't go.

Then, on December 19, Larry's birthday, Joe planned on seeing his dad as they had every year. But when he called Elisa, she had a new episode of *Where's Larry?* to report. In the latest installment, Larry the alcoholic had gone on a binge and was in a Malibu rehab, "And he's looking forward to seeing you," she told Joe. As she hung up, she said to him, "I love you sweetie."

A few days later, when Joe tried to get his birthday present to his father, Elisa had still another episode of *Where's Larry?* to offer him. She said Larry had left the rehab and was now out roaming the countryside ingesting drugs at a prolific pace.

Joe could not imagine a drug-crazed Larry escaping from rehab to pillage the countryside. He was disturbed not only by Elisa's contention that Larry was on drugs, but by her stories, which were wearing very thin.

"She was tripping on her lies, so I called my mom and said this woman must think I'm an idiot," he says.

Less than a week later, at Christmastime, Joe was supposed to go out to his dad's home to exchange Christmas presents with Haylei, Elisa, and his father, and he'd bought presents for all three of them. He called and Elisa answered the cell phone and offering yet another installment of *Where's Larry?* she informed him that Larry had gone on a binge and was perhaps in Reno, but they would get together. Elisa then called on Christmas Eve and said, "We have gifts."

"Cool," Joe said. "I've got presents too."

"We'll be by in an hour," Elisa said.

They never showed, and a few hours later Haylei called and said, "We'll be there in three hours."

Joe shook his head. He couldn't wait, and Elisa probably knew it. He had to make a three-hour drive to his mother's house to be there for Christmas day. "I said, no I gotta go and that's where we left it," Joe says.

By then Joe had heard enough, and he too checked in with the police department. That move did nothing to endear him to Elisa, who began to believe, and rightly so, that the vultures were circling her outpost at the McNabney home. Joe, Ginger, and Joyce were beginning to provide all the heat Elisa could handle.

At the start of the new year, an irate Elisa called Joe.

"Did you file a missing persons report on your dad?" she asked him point blank.

"Why? Is he missing?" Joe shot back.

"I don't know where he is," Elisa claimed. Then it was time for her latest edition of *Where's Larry?* "I think he's in Costa Rica or Washington," she said.

Joe was now not only angry, but confused. "Costa Rica? Washington? Elisa, what's going on?" he asked her. "First you say he's in rehab and now you say he's in Costa Rica? What's up?"

"I gotta go. I gotta go," she said quickly. "I have to go find your dad."

"If he's in Costa Rica, how are you going to find him?" Joe asked.

Unable to answer that question, Elisa hung up.

Meanwhile, Ginger was watching Elisa and the little world around her disintegrate at a rapidly accelerating pace. Joyce and Joe were adding to Elisa's woes, and the additional inquiries from bill collectors and other clients were sapping Elisa of her strength.

In the end, there were just too many people to juggle for Elisa and Sarah to keep up their act much longer. With her unique front row seat, Ginger watched as the whole thing came tumbling down. Elisa was also still under the influence of a healthy daily dose of alcohol, diet pills, and marijuana. So, when the mood struck her, or the chemicals moved her, she continued to drop little hints about Larry in her daily conversations with Ginger.

One day the two of them were alone in the office when Elisa suddenly volunteered that Larry used to call her daughter a "cunt" and that she "hated that sorry fucking bastard." In retrospect Ginger realized that it was no coincidence that she'd referred to Larry in the past tense.

The law firm was being run out of the McNabney home now, and Elisa was stripping the office of everything she could. Clients were calling asking for money, employees weren't getting paid, and at the height of this high drama, Elisa approached Ginger one day and told her with appropriate hubris that she was going to sell her BMW and get a new car, maybe a Porsche or another Jaguar. So she and Sarah went together to a Jaguar dealership in Sacramento. "They might have been husband and wife. They were together twenty-four hours a day," Ginger says of the two.

The pair left, and twenty minutes later they showed up with a new Jaguar. They had forged Larry's signature on his business account to pay for the lease.

Elisa also began to throw away a tremendous amount of things. "I've never seen people waste like they do," Ginger says. "I know there was some great stuff that anybody would have been more than happy to have. There were Channel pillows, like yellow ones and blue ones. That's not her color. She likes leopard print and red, which Larry would not have."

Ginger kept her mouth shut in front of Elisa, never confronting her about her missing boss, while keeping track of all the information and passing what she could to the police. "There was no Larry there," she says. "She was complaining about how much of an asshole he was and about how he tipped the bartender so much and made a scene in public. She was like not saying one good thing about Larry. A few days prior to that she was talking about how great things were and maybe they could get back together someday. Then it was rage. Her rage is scary because she's bad. I've never seen anyone that upset about stuff."

Sarah was a little better, but she was having her own problems too. She was still in college, and that fall she was taking an *ethics* class. She later told police it was her "worst semester" and the ethics class "drove me up the wall." This frustration was understandable considering the ethical dilemma she faced when she slowly poisoned a man to death. "I wonder if they discussed anything like that in her ethics class," one of the prosecutors in the case later mused.

Sarah said she was smoking marijuana to stay numb and forget what she had done to Larry in September. She claimed to have had trouble sleeping and eating, but all anyone saw of her was the party side. Meanwhile, she and Elisa continued to run through the money and bleed the law firm dry.

Also, they systematically began to sell off horses, trailers, and everything associated with the quarter horse endeavor Larry had painstakingly built up. His beloved Justa Lotta Page was sold, as was everything else. The money went straight into Elisa's pocket, and she and Sarah continued to spend lavishly with cash, avoided paying bills whenever possible, bounced checks when they could get away with it, and generally wrought havoc wherever they went.

Meanwhile, Joyce Blair Carter was pissed because Larry owed her money totaling nearly $150,000. She had checked with State Farm Insurance and discovered that the checks had been cut and made out to the

McNabney law firm. Elisa originally told her the checks were being held because of an IRS tax lien. When Joyce confronted Elisa, she gave Joyce $30,000 as an advance on the $150,000 and promised the rest "very soon." Joyce had been unconvinced, unswayed and sore about not getting the rest of her money. She went to the sheriff.

Ginger Miller had reported Larry missing. Joyce Blair Carter had not yet said that, but she reported some strange transactions in the McNabney law firm. And later Joe McNabney would add his voice to the rest, concerned about strange activities at the firm.

At first the police didn't know what they had. Larry could have been the victim of foul play, or he could have had Elisa running interference for him as he bilked his clients and took off with the money. No one knew for sure. That ambivalence was still there as late as February of 2002, when a local reporter said that an attorney had served McNabney papers in Acampo, a small town north of Lodi. The attorney filed suit against McNabney for forging his name in order to cash a settlement check.

It was Elisa or Sarah who'd forged the signature, but according to the attorney, McNabney had been hiding out and the attorney had found him. It was written up in *The Recorder,* a story about a local lawyer who split town with the money of his clients and other attorneys.

By the beginning of 2002 there was very little money left, and to make matters worse, the police had finally contacted Elisa about Larry. Ginger said Elisa was startled and frightened by the call: "She said that she couldn't believe that someone called a missing persons report in."

To compound matters, Ginger said Elisa claimed the missing persons report was not only unnecessary, but the direct result of Larry just being a lazy slob and not showing up to work or contacting his family. "She said this guy has caused her so many problems, she couldn't believe that he would do that. She said she was just going to tell him to get his lazy ass up and go over there and let them see him in person because she was sick of this shit," Ginger told police.

According to Ginger, Elisa then said she was supposed to go in to talk to police the next day, but she was going to send "Larry's ass in there."

The police were shocked to hear that Elisa was going to "go in tomorrow," meaning she would visit the police station. "We never talked to her," a confused police officer told Ginger.

Someone else in law enforcement had, though, and it put the fear of God into Elisa. Ginger saw her pack bras, clothes, shoes, and other personal effects into a plastic bag. Elisa told her she was going to a horse show in Arizona, and began loading the horse trailer full of everything but horses, most of which had already been sold off. Ginger knew it was a lie and suspected Elisa was getting ready to blow out of town.

"That was the last day," Ginger says.

Elisa was upset and packing quickly and furiously, mostly by herself because Sarah and Haylei were gone together somewhere. Elisa got angry with both of them when they returned, threw some more belongings in the back of her newly leased Jaguar, and the next day split out of town with her daughter in a cloud of dust.

Ginger and Sarah never saw Elisa again.

14

Where's My Dad?

On January 11, 2002, Joe McNabney finally came to the Sacramento sheriff's office to report his father missing. It had been many weeks since Ginger had stepped forward, and Joe at the time hadn't heard from his father for several months. He also had heard all the stories from Elisa that he could handle.

The *Where's Larry?* show was effectively cancelled.

Elisa had told Joe not to worry about Larry, but he wasn't listening to her. Because of things his father had told him about her, Joe suspected that not only was Elisa not telling the truth, but might have something to do with his father's disappearance.

It wasn't long before Elisa called him and confronted him on the issue. Ginger watched her on the phone, accusing Joe of calling in a missing persons report on his father, while Ginger knew all along she had been the one to get the ball rolling. She was grateful that Elisa didn't know it was her, and she vowed to keep it from Elisa as long as possible.

She heard Elisa tell Joe that cops had been out at the ranch looking for Larry because he'd been reported missing. She was trying to bully him, but Joe had an ace up his sleeve to play on Elisa. He had received a telephone call from an acquaintance who had found a belt buckle with Larry's name on it. The young woman found it near the abandoned law offices on Howe Avenue. When Joe asked Elisa about the buckle, she said she had been in the area looking for new office space and it had been in a box full of things she intended to throw away and it probably fell out.

"Your dad would be happy to hear you have the belt buckle," she told Joe. That didn't make a bit of sense to him, as Elisa had just said it was in a box of things to be thrown away. But before he could confront her on the issue, she abruptly said she had to go "find Larry" and hung up. Instead she hired a driver to take a horse trailer full of possessions to the horse show she planned to attend in Scottsdale, Arizona. It never made it. Thanks to Ginger Miller and others, police were beginning to get wise to Elisa's multitude of lies. The end was coming soon, and Elisa, with her preternatural instincts could smell it.

Joyce Blair Carter was doing her bit to bring on Elisa's demise. By following her and calling her constantly, and by keeping in touch with Ginger, she too began to think that Larry wasn't around. "I called up and asked Ginger if Larry had other clients that he owed money to like me," Joyce recalls. "He owed us about $150,000, and I couldn't imagine that any attorney would skip town just for that small amount of money, you know, putting your career and everything on the line for that. So, when Ginger told me that no, there weren't that many others, I thought, oh my God, he's dead."

When an IRS agent left a business card in the door of Elisa's home a few days later, she knew the time was ripe to get out of town. But she wouldn't go. Not yet anyway. Although the business card had put the fear of God in her, she was still going to plan her departure from California the way she wanted it. In those last few days, she desperately tried to put together a retirement or at least an "on the lam" package to take with her as she fled. But there was so little left. The newspapers would scream that she and Sarah had bilked the Mc-Nabney law firm for more than $500,000 after they killed Larry, which was probably true, but as the walls came crashing down during those finals days in January, there was precious little money left. It had all flowed through her hands like sand through a sieve. Elisa had nothing but some expensive jewelry, some cash, and the Jaguar. Her bankroll was too small for an extended foray through the countryside, and she didn't have enough to effectively flee the country. She didn't even worry about passports or IDs. If she had the money and was inclined to flee, then nothing as minuscule as the lack of proper identification could keep her from leaving the country.

After New Year's, as she assessed what she had, she came to one inescapable conclusion: She was going to have to get a job somewhere. She would have to eat, sleep, pay bills, care for her daughter, and try to settle down somewhere. It may have sounded like the very height of folly to believe that a woman on the run for murdering her husband could possibly entertain such thoughts, but Elisa had beaten the odds most of her life.

Besides, she'd gone from a size ten dress size to a size two. She'd cut and dyed her hair. She didn't look the same as she once had, and more important, when she made herself up, she didn't look like anyone on the run. Those who saw her during this time remarked about how well she looked. That probably had less to do with her care and grooming than with the fact that once she got out of the house she'd shared with a dead body for several months, she probably felt as if a huge weight had been lifted from her.

Elisa thought that the last six years could be wiped away and she could start over anew with her daughter. The bottom line with her and Haylei was that no matter who else spent time with her and who else she felt was her friend, when it came down to it, she was Laren Sims and her daughter was Haylei Sims Jordan. They had a past together and a bond stronger than anything else Elisa had in her life. So she would protect that to the best of her warped ability, and those who thought they knew her—including Sarah Dutra—really had no clue as to what she was all about.

In the end, it was only Haylei who mattered to her mother. Elisa could get angry with her daughter, and she could mislead her. She could lie to Haylei, and did often. Her battles with her daughter had almost taken on the status of legend in the law firm, but Haylei knew

Elisa better than anyone, and despite their trials and tribulations, loved her mother unconditionally. Elisa/Laren could never forget that. Haylei was the one pure thing in her life.

In the early part of January, Elisa left her landlord a message saying she was going to move soon because Larry needed extensive rehabilitation after his debilitating stroke. The house, she said, would be available by the end of the month.

On January 10 the McNabney law firm was toast and Elisa, along with Haylei, was gone. They planned to attend a horse show in Scottsdale, Arizona, and as Elisa planned for the trip, she also planned to leave town. Ginger Miller had seen her packing things and preparing to split, but Sarah thought she might be coming back, or at the very least would take her with her. But things were red hot around the McNabney homestead. Larry was finally gone and buried, but Joe, Joyce, and Ginger had called in the law, as had Tavia Williams. The screws were beginning to tighten, and Elisa had no intention of getting caught if she could avoid it.

Sarah, who'd once bragged to a college friend how she'd stolen from Elisa and taken her for a ride, then got taken for one herself. Elisa told her to show up at the Sacramento airport and said there would be a paid plane ticket for her there so Sarah could meet her in Scottsdale, Arizona, at the horse show she was allegedly attending.

When Sarah got to the airport, the ticket was there, all right, in her name, but unpaid. Sarah had no money. She looked up from the airline counter and panicked.

Then she tried to call Elisa on her cell phone, but it was disconnected.

For the next four hours Sarah tried desperately to get on a plane to Arizona to meet her soulmate, Elisa Mc-Nabney. They had been partners in crimes large and small, party friends, lovers—if you believe some reports—but at the very least a modern day version of Thelma and Louise, and Sarah thought the last reel would play out with the two by each other's side. It didn't happen that way. Sarah was alone and Elisa was gone, and at that moment Sarah had to know that Elisa had the last laugh on her. Elisa had ultimately used her as she'd used everyone else in her life, and when she used Sarah all up, Elisa threw her away in the busy Sacramento airport.

The next time Sarah would see Elisa was in an autopsy photo months later.

Meanwhile, Elisa had other things on her mind. She was running again with her daughter—not unfamiliar territory for her, but this time the stakes were higher. She didn't know how long she had before the police would be looking for her, nor did she have any idea how long Larry's body would remain buried, but she knew she had precious little time to get away, so she tried to make the most of it.

She didn't tell Haylei the truth of why they were running, not yet. As they took off and headed east, Elisa told her daughter that she and Larry were fleeing a nasty custody battle over her. It may not have made much sense, but Haylei had long ago grown smart enough not to question her mother's lies too closely. In some ways, Haylei was just happy to have her mother to herself again. Until the end, Elisa had the innate ability to light up a room and charm people. She was larger than life, and Haylei truly adored that quality in her mother and longed to bask in her glow.

As they headed east, she got her chance.

Meanwhile, others were hoping they could get as close to Elisa as Haylei was, but for other reasons. When she blew out of town for the Scottsdale, Arizona, horse show, there is every indication that she intended to go with more than the clothes on her back. She had packed the horse trailer full of possessions, computers, clothes, and mementos. But, tipped off by Ginger and others, the police were able to confiscate and later search it. Some thought the police might find Larry stashed in the trailer, but they didn't, and the police also found few, if any, clues that could tell them what happened to Larry.

Meanwhile, the big fish had gotten away. The police wanted to snatch Elisa and question her about Larry's disappearance as well as the financial shenanigans at the law firm, but then they found out that she'd blown out of town in the little red Jaguar with a tan roof. That piqued their curiosity, and finding Elisa suddenly became paramount to discovering what had happened to Larry.

The police then told the local papers that other information had recently become known to them that further heightened their interest—such as the fact that Elisa had sold the couple's luxury Ford pickup truck for a discounted $27,000 just after her husband disappeared; that she was believed to be headed to Scottsdale, Arizona, where Laurence McNabney had made a name for himself on the quarter horse show circuit; that she had tried to ship the couple's $100,000 horse trailer loaded with personal belongings to Scottsdale recently, until sheriff's deputies confiscated it.

Police had also talked to some people, who, as it turned out, would be key witnesses. Mary Whalen, the wife of Greg Whalen, Larry's horse trainer, told the police she'd contacted the credit bureau because someone had attempted to take out two credit cards in the Whalens' name and were denied. What was even more disturbing to Mary was the fact that the person trying to open the accounts had done so in her mother's maiden name. Then Mary remembered that Elisa, during a visit to their home, had asked a lot of questions. It had been a simple, friendly conversation, but had steered the talk around to her and Greg's heritage, and the maiden names of both their mothers.

She felt the hair rise on the back of her neck.

The implication was that Elisa had tried to steal from one of her dearest friends. Mary and Greg had become close to the McNabneys, especially as the success of their collaborative efforts on the quarter horse circuit began to pay dividends. Being on the team with Larry McNabney and his meteoric rise in the quarter horse show arenas across the country gave Mary and Greg a sense of comfort and trust with Larry and his wife. It was a sudden and hard slap in the face for Mary Whalen to think that Elisa could deceive her.

Mary joined a club whose other members included Ken Redelsperger, Larry McNabney, and scores of others who'd mistakenly trusted Elisa over the years.

The deceit was far from over, and the Whalens found themselves trying desperately to keep their heads above the crashing waves of accusations and injuries that came as a result of their brief friendship with Elisa.

Almost immediately after Mary Whalen told the police about her stolen credit cards, other evidence came out that could have made it seem that Elisa and Greg Whalen were willing co-conspirators. Witnesses came forward who said they saw Greg and Elisa sharing an intimate moment together in a passionate kiss and embrace at one of the horse shows.

Greg was interviewed and denied being intimately involved with Elisa. But he did admit that on *one* occasion a worker from his ranch had gone to the Woodbridge house of Elisa and Larry McNabney to remove some furniture.

By then police became interested in finding a refrigerator that was reported to have been in the McNabney garage. But along with most of the rest of the furniture and fixtures, it had recently disappeared. Whalen denied he removed the refrigerator. Another worker came forward who said that Greg Whalen had lied, that indeed there had been more than one visit to the Woodbridge home and the refrigerator *had* been removed by Whalen's workers—at his request. According to Cipriano Rios, the ranch foreman at Blue Ribbon Farms, Greg Whalen's ranch, Greg told him not to tell anyone that he'd visited the Woodbridge home. Apparently, Greg was doing a favor for Elisa.

With that information, the police faced a couple of prospects. If the other witnesses were telling the truth, then Greg Whalen might indeed have been Elisa's co-conspirator. Then again, as they came to know more about Elisa, they also entertained the ultimately more probable scenario of Elisa taking advantage of an unknowing and unsuspecting older gentleman who was innocently smitten with her. Getting along with any man at any age, with the exception of her own father, never seemed to be a major problem for Elisa. It was, in fact, one of her greatest talents.

The California authorities were still calling Laren by her Elisa McNabney alias at that time, because they didn't know she had changed her name. While they had a physical description of her and the car, they quickly found that nothing existed on paper that could identify her. She didn't have a California driver's license, she had more than one set of phony Social Security numbers and she had no credit cards in her name. She was a paper ghost. People saw her often enough, but there was precious little in the public records to prove she ever existed.

She did have her daughter Haylei with her, and in the beginning that was cause for some concern as the two took off from California. Police found a phone number and the name of Jennifer Brakett among papers they believed belonged to Haylei. They called Jennifer and she told them that she and Haylei had been "closer than sisters" since Haylei was thirteen or fourteen years old and that the two had run up "big phone bills" talking to one another during the last few years. They had rarely gone more than a week without talking or exchanging e-mails or letters, so Jennifer was concerned about Haylei.

Elisa later told police that she had often feared for Haylei when Larry was around because he was so caustic to her daughter, but that wasn't a concern of Haylei's, at least according to Jennifer. She said that Haylei loved Larry McNabney and that he treated her like a daughter. Jennifer said Haylei never told her anything about Larry threatening Haylei's life. But within the last few months Haylei had told her friend that Elisa and Larry were divorced and that Larry had joined a cult "but was happy."

Police thought there was cause for concern over Haylei's health since she disappeared with her mother, but again this only showed how little they knew at the time. Laren had no plans to harm her child. As dark as her desires were, Laren fully intended to use them not only for her own survival, but to slip away quietly and care for her daughter.

She was a vapor trail. "She was very, very good," said detective Deborah Scheffel, who investigated the case. "I've tracked a lot of criminals, but she was one of the best con artists I've ever run across. She was not a stupid woman."

When Laren hit the road, shedding her Elisa McNabney alias, which she'd carried off so well for the previous six years, she knew things were going to be tough. She had no idea how tough, but she knew she would have to find a way to feed the appetite she'd developed for cash.

With all of those worries, it was also possible for her in some way to find a little corner of happiness. It was her and Haylei alone, again, for one thing. If she could black out the heinous activities of the last few months, Laren could also find herself happy to be on the road again. It was where she survived the best—having to constantly think on her feet and at the same time not have the stress of a husband, law firm, laws, and parasitic friends like Sarah.

Finally burying Larry had allowed her to breathe freely and to finally shed the turgid mess she'd made of things in California. The bill collectors, the threats, the angry clients like Joyce Blair Carter and others. All of them were a nuisance to her and nothing more. In the end even her friendship to Sarah was something she happily shed.

Meanwhile, Sarah had no place to run. It was back to school and her tough ethics class. Incredibly, three days after Elisa split, she contacted Ginger Miller and, Ginger claimed, told her that she was going to "find a new job because the business wasn't doing good and Elisa is giving up on it. I asked if I should be looking for a new job, and she said she wasn't going to tell me that. I told her that I don't know what to tell her, that if I heard something I would let her know. She said, 'Please give me your phone number.' She's a bad person, I've known what she's done, and I don't want to associate with her."

Ginger was amazed that Sarah would be contacting her trying to find work: "She asked *me* to help *her* find a job."

Sarah was out of work, beginning to panic, and wondering not if, but when, her participation in Larry's murder would become known and how she could wiggle out of it. Since Elisa had dumped her, it quickly became apparent to Sarah that the best way to handle any heat was to deflect it to Elisa. Sarah knew Elisa couldn't squirm out of it because while she returned to her rather normal life before being involved with Larry McNabney, Elisa had hit the road.

If she played her cards right, she thought, she could position herself as another one of Elisa's unwitting victims.

Laren didn't care. She'd shed her Elisa skin when

she fled California. In her mind she'd already put that life behind her. What she couldn't shed was the impending feeling of doom and dread she felt every time she saw a police car or heard a telephone ring. A case in point was something that occurred not long after she fled with her daughter.

They were driving in the evening through one of the western states when she got pulled over by the police. She was as scared as she'd ever been in her life. She didn't know what to expect. Was there a warrant for her? There was. Had Larry's body been found? All she knew was that if the police officer pulling her over decided to check her credentials, or check the license plates on her car, she was very likely headed for jail. But, as her parents said, even with her back against the wall, Laren was a very cool customer.

As the police officer approached her, she turned on the charm. From the cop's point of view, she was a woman who had driven a little too fast. She had what appeared to be her daughter in a red Jaguar, tan top down, and perhaps the pair were on a joy ride. They didn't look too threatening. The woman was dressed nicely, as was the young girl with her. Her manner was calm and easy. She didn't seem nervous, and she was very friendly. The appearance presented was not of a coldhearted murderer on the run from justice. In short there was nothing threatening about the two.

From Laren's point of view, the cop was simply someone to be controlled, and she'd had a lifetime of practice doing that.

"You don't want to see my identification" was what she said subtly with her body language, smile, and disarming demeanor. The charm worked on the police officer.

"Move along. Have a nice day."

And then she was gone.

A simple check of the license plate through the computer would have stopped Laren's flight from justice almost as soon as it had begun, but she and Haylei slipped the noose.

Back in Sacramento, just a few days after Elisa fled, Sarah was having her first meeting with the police and it finally dawned on her that she might be a patsy for everything that had gone wrong. After all, she was the one left holding the bag. But Sarah had no intention of going gentle into that good night, even if Elisa had planned it that way. Sarah had learned well under Elisa's tutelage.

Sarah told police that she indeed worked for the McNabney law firm and had since sometime in 2000. She admitted Elisa was a friend of hers and that she had shared an apartment with her daughter Haylei. But most of what she told police that day was riddled with holes. She told them that the last time she saw Larry was at the horse show in Industry City and that he and Elisa seemed to be getting along just fine.

According to Sarah, Elisa had told her that Larry was doing heroin and any drugs he could get his hands on. However, she said she only saw Larry drinking wine and never anything stronger. It was a subtle attempt to make sure the police focused their attention on Elisa without making them suspicious of her. Otherwise, in her first interview Sarah tried to remain somewhat true to Elisa. She did volunteer that Elisa told her Larry had asked for a divorce and that was why she had leased the red Jaguar for Elisa in her name; Elisa didn't want Larry to get anything in the divorce settlement.

In Sarah's version of *Where's Larry?* the divorce was the reason Elisa never reported Larry missing. Sarah said Elisa believed Larry would eventually surface; he'd been served the divorce papers and then fled, perhaps on a binge or an extended vacation. And it was Elisa who was the major money-maker in the relationship, Sarah said. Elisa did all the work, settling cases and dealing with adjusters—even though she held no law degree. Elisa was at work every day in Sarah's story, and Larry never lifted a finger to help.

Sarah didn't have to give up Elisa in the first interview, because she still didn't know what Elisa planned to do. By offering only what she felt she had to give the police, she hoped to keep her options open.

Sarah told the Sacramento sheriff's office that Elisa had sent her to rent a wheelchair at the Industry City horse show, but that she knew precious little else about what went on. At the end of the interview she volunteered a little more information about Elisa and the wheelchair. In this version of the story, Larry was drunk and waving his arms as Elisa rolled him away in the wheelchair and into his pickup truck. She returned twenty minutes later without him.

Meanwhile, out on the road, Laren had shed her Elisa alias and became Shane Ivaroni, among other names. Melissa Gobbler was another favorite, and on occasion Sarah Dutra or Elisa Barasch. She first headed to Denver, and then found herself, of all places, in Louisville, Kentucky. Home of the Kentucky Derby, horse country like no other and a place where she felt she could do some serious damage.

Louisvillians love to pride themselves on their knowledge of fast horses, beautiful women, and a good Southern bourbon. But probably ten in the town of close to half a million people had ever seen anything like Floridian Laren Sims before.

Using all the charm she could muster, Laren blew into town looking for a lifeline, and found she had to pawn whatever jewelry she had to make ends meet and keep herself going on the road with Haylei.

Gary Asher got to meet her as she walked into his Celebrity Pawnshop on Preston Highway. Located not far from the airport, in a blue-collar end of Louisville, the pawnshop sits in a strip mall near stores like Town and Country Ford and Target. How Laren came to find the place is unknown, but when she sauntered in she had Gary's attention.

"I still have the jewelry she pawned," he says. "She was just a big smile and made a move on me. If I hadn't just been married, I'd've taken her up on her offer. She was very good-looking and very enticing. She looked good in the Jaguar."

But she didn't stay in Louisville, although she found something familiar in the Southern hospitality and it must have focused her attention. She found herself drawn farther south—to Mississippi, and ultimately home to Florida.

While Laren was flirting with the pawnshop owner

in Louisville, the police in Sacramento were still trying to figure out who she was and what was going on.

She hadn't made it easy on them. Since departing California, she'd taken on a series of new aliases, conned anyone she met, and skittered across the country like a water spider using the surface tension of a pond. After the fact, detectives traced her activities through at least one homeless shelter in the Midwest where she looked for handouts of shoes and clothes.

The sheriff's detectives in California had confiscated the horse trailer in an attempt to find out more about her. They found computers, clothing, furniture, photographs, and even dishes, according to Detective Steven Van Meter. "We will be very meticulous. We are very interested in discovering any information that will help us determine what happened," Van Meter told the local paper.

The police and the press were still referring to Laren as "Elisa," because they *still* had no idea who she was, and they were questioning anyone and everyone they could to figure out what had happened.

In San Joaquin County, where Larry's body was eventually found, authorities had been in contact with a man who owned a storage lot. Larry McNabney had been one of the names on a list of renters who owed him money for months. Nigel Travis, the manager at Public Storage, was about to auction off the contents of the storage locker when he saw Larry's name mentioned on television in a missing persons report. His jaw dropped and he called the police.

San Joaquin County authorities told Travis that they

would happily search Larry McNabney's storage
locker with a proper warrant. Until then they didn't
want it opened. The thought of Larry being stored inside a locker was a possibility detectives shuddered to
think about, yet it was a possibility. At the very least,
there was hopefully some evidence in the locker that
could help them find out where Larry was and what
had happened to his wife, not to mention who she really was. Travis said he had not seen what was in the
storage space, and upon police request he bolted the
door closed until they could get there.

Because police believed, and rightly so, that Laren
had fled the state, they called in the FBI to help find
her. It would seem a task that could be accomplished,
and it was, but not without a lot of leg and foot work.
While at first glance it appeared a fairly routine task for
the FBI to find a good-looking woman with a daughter
in a red Jaguar tooling around the countryside on the
run for murder, it wasn't that simple. As the FBI noted,
though the woman who was the focus of the investigation left behind a trail of debts and aliases, there was
little else that explained who she was and where she
might be. She changed her hair color and hairstyle like
others change their underwear. She had more than one
Social Security number and a decade-long track record
of avoiding the law.

Again, she would not go gentle into that good night.

Those left behind were getting a good taste of the
real nature of Laren Sims as well, and it wasn't sweet.
At the magazine for the Pacific Coast Quarter Horse
Association, Elisa and Larry left behind unpaid adver-
tising bills. Virginia McClintock, editor of the monthly

publication based in Temecula, told local reporters that when Larry's horses were winning, as they often did, he and his wife took out large, splashy ads to announce their accomplishments with pride. But, as she had also done with a lot of other bills, Laren stopped paying the magazine, and in turn they stopped listing Larry's horses in show results rosters.

Others involved in the horse trade also ran afoul of the Laren factor in their business. A photographer and graphic designer claimed the two owed him several thousand dollars in unpaid bills. A few people, once they found out that Larry's wife had left town, came forward with tragic tales of Larry's last days. He was leading the nation in the amateur division for his horse's age group in the halter class and had a chance to "win it all." And then there were those who said they had seen things they thought were suspicious, but only in retrospect.

By now Larry's children had hired a private investigator to help find their missing father, and Tavia, Joe, and Cristin became increasingly worried he'd never come home. "It's like a bad novel that you can't put the book down or a movie you can't walk out of," Tavia said.

Finally, a few days into the new year, the police made some progress figuring out who Elisa McNabney was.

"We've found some fingerprints, but we don't know if they're hers and which ones aren't," a San Joaquin County detective said. The cops found several Social Security numbers they say she used, though they didn't know if any were really hers. But they had found a Social Security number for a woman in Florida who was a former convict with a similar name: Elizabeth Barasch.

Time was running out on Laren, and while she didn't know it, her preternatural instincts kept her at least one step ahead of the detectives. She found herself in Biloxi, Mississippi, just as the police in California began to piece her identity together. But she wouldn't stay there long. Her luck would turn on her in Mississippi and finally force her hand. After years of being on the run, after the time she'd spent deceiving everyone she knew—even herself—her lies were finally spread too thin.

In the South, her problems finally came home to roost. Laren had nowhere else she could run. Soon, for the first time in nearly a decade, she would find herself in her home state of Florida. She would get anything but a warm reception.

16

I'm the One You're Looking For

Destin, Florida, sits on a peninsula on the Florida panhandle far away from the heavy traffic of the Atlantic coast and of course still farther away from the mess Laren left behind in California. But the town, while isolated, is not forgotten. The local paper boasts that Destin is the playground for movie stars and celebrities who like the comforts of home but not the crowds. The city boosters like to call the area Florida's "Emerald Coast," and they talk about rubbing elbows with everyone from John Grisham to Britney Spears.

It's also a military town, with Eglin Air Force Base nearby, and it was the perfect resort for Laren in her flight from justice. Around ten thousand people live in Destin, which consists mostly of quiet streets, condos, parasailing shops, and some tiny tourist attractions. There are tattoo parlors, the occasional Krispy Kreme doughnut shop, small grocery stores, a pizza parlor, and the essential Chinese restaurant. The town bills itself as "the World's Luckiest Fishing Village," and it seemed a perfect place for Laren to try her luck.

At the end of January she ran into a large jovial man at a Biloxi, Mississippi, golf tournament. Jonathan Holland* admired her Jaguar, and she pretended to admire his. They shared drinks in a casino while Haylei was left in a hotel room. Then the pair moved to the craps table, where Laren's newfound friend won $3,000.

"I believe in Lady Luck," Jonathan told a reporter. "So, I gave her a couple hundred dollars."

Laren said she was an attorney thinking of opening up a practice in Biloxi, but Jonathan recommended Destin, Florida. He ran a furniture store in Destin and offered her a chance to stay at a beach house he had there. Any time she wanted to come by, he said, she should just drop right on in.

She was back in business. Her flight from Florida had taken her cross-country, and she'd been gone for more than nine years. But by the end of January, just a few days after meeting a kind furniture store owner, she was back in the state where she was born. She returned in style too. Her new friend had a Pelican Beach Resort condo overlooking the water, and Haylei and Laren stayed there while both looked for work.

Years of living lavishly had spoiled them both, and Laren didn't want to go back to homeless shelters begging for meals and shoes. Naturally, she got a job quickly. By the first week of February she was working

---

*Not his real name.

at Destin Chops, an expensive upscale steak house. Locals wait months, sometimes longer, to get a job at the steak house. Not Laren. Declaring herself a wine connoisseur, she walked in and got a job on the spot.

About that time, another wine connoisseur was finally found after not being seen for months. A migrant worker walking the long row of grapes in the vineyard near Larry McNabney's home saw what appeared to be a human leg sticking out of the ground. Pale and tattered, it most definitely didn't belong to someone alive. The worker got help, and soon police were swarming the area, excavating the body.

They were soon convinced it was Larry McNabney, but they couldn't figure out why he was so well-preserved. He had last been seen, and was suspected to have been murdered, sometime around September 10, 2001. He'd been in the ground for five months. Some suggested a freezer, but that would rupture and destroy the cells, so when the body thawed it would be a horrible mess.

Then, someone suggested refrigeration. "She stuck his ass in a refrigerator," one of the cops said. "Can you imagine it?"

While Larry McNabney was being identified and an autopsy performed, his ex-wife, now going by the name of Shane Ivaroni, was finishing up at the steak house. Three days after Larry's body was found, Laren found a new job. While waiting tables at the steak house, which was a favorite haunt for local attorneys, she made a new friend, Paul Lydolph, a twenty-nine-year-old local lawyer with a promising future. He saw Laren, spoke with her, and felt inclined to hire her as a part-time legal assistant at the firm where he was a partner. There would be no question about Laren getting a job, any job she wanted, because people just didn't turn her down. Even as she was on the run for murder, even as her husband's body was being exhumed and identified, and even as the FBI was getting into the case, Laren Sims was settling in at a new law firm. Haylei got a job too, and began working at a small restaurant in a shopping center where Jonathan Holland had his furniture store.

Meanwhile, things were coming to a head in California. Investigators still didn't know who Elisa was, so they were tripping over themselves trying to interview former friends, trying to find her former husband Ken Redelsperger and to sort through the convoluted mess that was her life from the time she fled Florida in the early nineties. Only, no one seemed to knew who she was and where she came from. For almost two months after Laren was gone, the only thing police knew for sure was that she'd fled town and was last seen in a red Jaguar with her daughter, whose age was listed as anywhere from sixteen to nineteen years old. Laren had covered her tracks well, but her luck was about up.

Extensive testing was done on Larry's body, and hair samples showed that he may have been slowly poisoned over a period of about three months. This would be consistent with the return of Sarah Dutra from the extended student exchange trip to Italy. But the same tests could have been skewed by the fact that during the decomposition of Larry's body, his hair was contaminated by body fluids tainted with the poison that killed him.

Greg Whalen was also experiencing his own bad luck at the time. Cipriano Rios, the foreman at his ranch, had come forward to say that Greg had lied about how many times workers had gone from the ranch to empty out furniture and other possessions at the McNabneys' Woodbridge home. In the first week of January 2002, Whalen sent Rios to help Elisa move some items into a U-Haul truck. Rios, another worker, and that man's five-year-old son got a tabletop, toolbox with tools, and an electric fan as payment, as well as some of Larry's clothes. Rios said that Greg Whalen told him not to tell the authorities that he had helped move items in the house, a move that would have disastrous consequences for Whalen later.

Forty-eight-year-old Bob Murphy met Laren about that time. They struck up a casual friendship, and when he got tickets to a Kid Rock concert in New Orleans on March 9, he invited her to come along.

Angie DeSimone, a new acquaintance of Laren's, who also went to the concert with them that night, remembered Laren very well and talked to reporters about it afterward. "I was so excited about going," she said. "I told her I never get to go anywhere."

Laren responded, "Me either."

DeSimone said Laren looked extremely tired and spent a lot of time lying on her bed in her New Orleans hotel room. "She looked a lot older than me," DeSimone says. "She looked like she had been out of lotion for a while."

Truth was, she was out of just about everything. Desperate, tired, and barely able to function, Lauren was operating just a few short steps ahead of the law, and with her sense of danger, she knew the police were closing in on her. Indeed the authorities in California had issued a warrant for her arrest, even though they still didn't know her real name.

While Lauren was away at the concert, Jonathan opened his credit card bill to find an extra $1,000 in charges at a Winn Dixie supermarket and the Gap, among other places. A cell phone had been taken out under the name of his furniture business, and it had a $100 charge. Laren had struck again. But this time someone struck back. Jonathan changed the locks on the condo he'd loaned to Laren and Haylei, cleaned out the clothes left behind by both mother and daughter, and also got rid of Haylei's brand new pet albino rat. Among the clothes thrown out were swimsuits, underwear, towels, and about a dozen pairs of black shoes.

Just a few short weeks in Florida after her flight from California, and despite having all of her worldly possessions confiscated when her horse trailer was nabbed by authorities, Laren was already rebuilding her stock and reclaiming her place in society. She only needed to find another willing host to suit her needs and she had a couple of likely prospects.

For now, getting back from the concert, she and Haylei moved into a motel, and then stayed with a mutual friend.

On March 13 police in California finally got a break. The FBI had found an address for Elizabeth Barasch, the first name Laren had used when she met Ken Redelsperger. Showing up at the Barasch home in West Palm Beach, they hoped to find Laren. Instead they found the real Elizabeth Barasch who had no idea what the police were babbling about. Then someone said "con artist" and showed her a picture. "I know that woman," the real Elisa said. She'd spent time with her in prison in 1991. Her name was Laren Sims.

"We finally had something, and it was a big one," said Deborah Scheffel. "The woman had done a very good job at hiding who she really was for a very long time."

Once Laren's identity was established, detectives were dispatched to Brooksville to talk to Jesse and Jackie, who were still living in their log home north of town. They said they hadn't seen their daughter for nearly ten years and often wondered and worried about what had happened to the second of their four children. "You can imagine a mother's concern when police show up and want to know about your daughter that you haven't seen in such a long time," Jackie later said.

"I didn't know what to think," she now says, "but I was worried. I still love her."

The police weren't in love with her, but they were in love with the idea that they might be close to catching her.

Then they caught another break. Jonathan Holland decided to drop in at the local law firm where Laren was employed and have a few words with her boss, Paul Lydolph, who'd hired her on the spot at the local steak house. He had a few choice things to tell Lydolph about his brand new secretary, and none of them were good.

Jonathan was especially irked to learn Laren had used his stolen credit card to purchase lunch for the four people in Bob Murphy's car upon their return from the Kid Rock concert.

On March 14 it all came crashing down. Laren got to work at the office, but for some reason suspected something was up. No one can say why she thought so. Perhaps, like one of Anne Rice's vampires, she had heightened senses. Everyone in the office at the time thought they were playing it cool. They had checked her Social Security number and discovered that it belonged to a man. While she was at work that morning, someone snuck out the back and got the vehicle identification number from her Jaguar.

For the detectives in California, it was almost unbelievable. They had found Laren Sims, and guess what she was doing—working in another law firm in her home state as a legal secretary. For some it seemed like the world had been turned upside down. "How could she keep getting work?" one of the investigators asked. "Didn't anyone ever hear of a background check?"

With Laren, logic never applied. When she told her employers that she was going to the doctor, for instance, they believed her. They didn't have any reason to suspect that Elisa knew they'd figured her out. But she'd caught a whiff of something at the law firm and knew they were on to her.

She didn't go to the doctor.

Instead she called up Bob Murphy.

"Whatcha doing?" she asked in her best little girl voice.

"Got no plans," he said.

Then suddenly he did. Laren came over, leaving Haylei once again to fend for herself with her own friends while her mother searched for a fresh host to feed upon.

Laren never went back to work. Instead she went out with Bob to see the Mel Gibson movie *We Were Soldiers*. Then they went to dinner, rented some videos, and finally ended the evening back at Bob's place. He paid for everything because, he said, he was just "that kind of guy."

Laren never tired of "that type of guy," and could take advantage of them quicker than she could bed them. Since she knew time was running out, she didn't have the luxury of staying with Bob for months while she slowly bled him. The next morning when Murphy woke up, he found that Laren was gone, as was his green Dodge Dakota pickup truck and $600 in cash. But Laren had been sweet enough to leave him a note explaining her good intentions. "I took your money, I took your truck. I'll be back," the note said.

Flabbergasted, angry, hurt, and bewildered, Bob walked outside and found Laren's red Jaguar with the keys waiting for him in the front seat. Oh well, it didn't seem like such a bad trade as all that—until he got to work and found that the police wanted to talk to him about his new friend, and by the way, they also wanted to confiscate the car.

Bob had no idea what he had run across when he connected up with Laren Sims, and he was so grateful that he got out of it as easily as he did that he didn't even want to press charges against her. In her subsequent confession to police, Laren expressed some remorse at taking Bob's money, but said he had willingly loaned her the car and the cash. She added that he was such a nice guy, and she was grateful he didn't press charges. In saying what she did to police about that incident, she showed more concern for a total stranger than she ever showed for her own husband, who'd supported her and stood between her and all of her enemies for those many years in California.

Laren's luck had held again. The police later estimated that they missed her by less than an hour when she left the law office near Destin, Florida. One hour. She had escaped by the narrowest of margins.

She had picked up Haylei, took off out of town, and was last seen traveling north.

Monday, March 18, 2002, marked the last day of freedom for Laren Sims. After leaving Destin, police say mother and daughter headed to Charleston, South Carolina, for the weekend. But Laren had noticed that in the brief time they spent in Destin, Haylei had made some friends her own age, and they seemed to be good people. Haylei had even met a boyfriend she was fond of, and she begged her mother to let her say good-bye to him.

Finally, and ultimately, the guilt came crashing down on Laren. She turned the car around and drove back to Florida, not so much because she wanted to silence her daughter's demands, but because she just didn't have anyplace else to run and no energy left with which to do it. Or perhaps she was responding to her daughter, and if there was a noble effort in anything that she did, it was at that moment.

Laren had rarely thought of anyone but herself, and it would be nice to believe that it was the pleading of her child who begged for a "normal life like everyone else" that got to her, not just the fear and the exhaustion of being on the lam for a better part of a decade. In fact, she finally broke down and told Haylei the truth about everything, including killing Larry. For Laren, it was an act of submission, a waving of the white flag. She was drained by the experience. Almost calm.

Haylei was floored, shocked, and saddened by her mother's admission. She hadn't been fond of Sarah for a long time, and when her mother told her that Sarah was involved in Larry's death, it became easier for her to dislike Sarah even more.

When Laren got to town on that Monday, she dropped Haylei off at her friends' and then left. People in town saw the pickup truck she'd taken and alerted the police. Haylei was picked up by the police about nine-thirty p.m. that night, and then investigators got "all the deputies that we could" and began searching the area. They were stunned that Laren had returned to town, but were determined to catch her before she decided to leave again. Haylei also wanted to see her mother captured, because she had never seen her mother so despondent before. She told police that she thought Laren might kill herself.

About fifteen minutes later police found the pickup truck abandoned at the local Winn Dixie near the beach. A checkout girl said she watched Laren park the truck and then wander across the highway to the beach.

She was playing out her last scene of freedom, with drama and a flourish. Wearing a red jacket and blue jeans, she strolled aimlessly across the beach alone, then found a chair to sit in. When a deputy spotted her, she looked as if she hadn't a care in the world. She was apparently relaxing, enjoying the breeze, the water, and the sand. As the deputy approached cautiously, she rose quickly and walked over to meet him.

"Can I see some identification please?" the deputy asked, startled that the object of his surveillance was aware of his presence.

Laren probably had to suppress a smile or a laugh. She hadn't had any real identification in so long; she probably didn't even know what it looked like. She could have pulled out something that would convince the deputy she was Princess Diana, but the irony was, she had nothing that could betray her true identity. She didn't bother. She was done playing games.

"Yes, I'm the one you're looking for," she said in the little girl voice she sometimes used.

And just like that, with no struggle, no strong words, no fight left in her, and no desire to run anymore, Laren Sims was taken into custody. A letter she had written to Haylei was found in the pickup truck.

Laren Sims's decade-long flight from the law was over, and for once she was going to have to pay the bill when it came due.

17

Don't Kill My Dog!

Giving up on the beach was as natural for Laren as taking a breath, and just as easy. A weight had been lifted from her shoulders. There were no more decisions to make, no more control to exercise, save one last act, and the curtain was going up on that soon enough. But until then she had some things to put in order.

Once she was in jail, Laren didn't have to worry about what to wear for the first time in years, or where her next meal would come from, or where she would sleep. She was in a womb of care and her sigh of relief came in the form of her confession.

The day she was captured, police sat down with Laren for three hours, and spoke to her about Larry McNabney, her life on the run, Sarah Dutra, her daughter Haylei, and everything else she wanted to talk about, and Laren spoke at great length. Some of it was the truth, and chilling at that, while other parts of it were pure Laren blarney and spin control. Like a politician, she couldn't avoid the pretense—even when faced with life in prison.

To many who saw the videotape and read the confession, it was another attempt by Laren Sims, the actress, to write a movie in her head and perform it for an audience. But it also turned out to be potentially important evidence in the subsequent trial of Sarah Dutra. Her defense attorney, Kevin Clymo, argued that Laren's confession should be thrown out and that Laren was trying to "burn" Sarah in it, but prosecutor Tom Testa disagreed.

"We have already had a hearing on this when Elisa McNabney made her statement in Florida," Testa said. "She expressed concern for Sarah's welfare. 'How is Sarah doing? I'm glad she's okay.' The court remembers that. And she also went out of her way to say, 'No, Sarah did not help me bury the body.' If she were going to burn Sarah, that would be the time to do it."

He also pointed out exactly how Sarah did help Elisa, at least according to Laren's confession.

One of the first things Laren did was set the record straight about her identity. She began with pure record-keeping facts, outlining some of her many aliases to the police and the alternate birth dates she used on different IDs. "How do you keep track of this? That would just kill me," the officer taking her confession said.

"I've been running for nine years," Laren said matter-of-factly.

After going through some of the preliminaries of an interrogation, Laren began disclosing the aliases she'd used over the years, including Shane Ivaroni, Melissa

Gobler, Tammy Keelin, Elizabeth Barasch, Elisa or Elizabeth Redelsperger, and Elisa McNabney. Then she discussed the immediate past. She saw the policeman on the beach and approached him herself. There were kids there, she said, and she didn't want to frighten them, and she figured the police were coming for her anyway, so she initiated the contact.

"I mean, I knew that something needed to happen, either I needed to put a bullet in my head, or I needed to deal with it . . . Did I kill my husband? Yes, I killed my husband," she said point-blank, but it wasn't something the police were ready for just yet.

In fact, it took her interviewer by surprise. "Well, I don't want to get into that right now," the interviewer said. "I'm glad you didn't hurt yourself though, really."

But more important, the officer had yet to read Laren her Constitutional rights. By jumping the gun with an admission of murder, Laren could have put her confession in jeopardy at her subsequent trial, and the police wanted to avoid that possibility. So the female officer talking to Laren dutifully read her the Miranda rights, Laren dutifully waived her right to have an attorney present, and the officer commended her on doing the right thing.

Laren then let the police know that she had washed the truck she'd recently stolen, and the interviewer commended her for that as well, saying the man from whom Laren had stolen the truck wasn't going to press charges. Laren found some comfort in that, even though she was facing a murder charge, felony flight, and a host of other charges stemming from her nine years as a fugitive.

Then she slipped back into the same old routines she displayed as Elisa McNabney. Her felonious behavior was never far from the surface, and she used it to her benefit to try and squirm out of a possible death sentence. Laren's father had said she could never face a bill when it came due, and she wasn't about to start at that late date, if she could avoid it.

She told the police that she met Larry, eventually married him on February 6, 1995, and told him that "I had credit card fraud and all that, checks and dealings with stolen property . . . and I don't know if you guys do any history on the victim or not, but he had an alcohol and drug problem." Then she said that Larry "started hitting me July 2, 1995, and my daughter was in the house and I didn't want to make any waves . . . and he would say, you know, 'You can't leave me. If you leave me, I'm going to make sure that they take Haylei from you, you know.' "

Life was hell with Larry after he hit her and his drug intake escalated, she said. He used coke, meth, smoked heroin, took Special K, "whatever there is you know," and he was indiscriminately mean and vindictive. "He would stay in the room, drinking and watching porno and snorting coke, and so I would work . . . so I thought, well, I'd get him a horse, and that'll make him have something to do, 'cause he never worked."

At that point Laren felt it necessary to let the police know, "I'm just telling you guys the truth," which, one cop said later, was a "sure indication she probably wasn't."

Then she went on to outline how it was Larry who began taking money out of trust accounts and spending it wildly, not her, and how the business was suffering because they weren't generating any clients and how her life became a miserable hell. "He just starts getting mad, and I would wake up and he'd be choking me, or it was the drugs, it wasn't him. It was the drugs, and I would be like, you know, freaked out and scared."

But her torment from the evil of Larry didn't end there. According to Laren, he was constantly bringing hookers into the home, forcing her to put Haylei in a boarding school to protect her from the Ozzy Osbourne–like character careening through her house on a drunken, libidinous rampage.

There were drugs and bottles and remnants of his affairs with hookers strewn throughout the house. Laren even claimed one of the horse trainers found a big bag of heroin in a golf bag Larry gave away. She said it was "just horrible" living under those conditions with Larry.

He was on a rampage so devoid of logic that when he got caught by the police on a drunk driving charge, he ran through the home, unable to control himself, while she shouted to him, "Larry, you need to get your shit together. The cops are on their way and you are going to jail."

Unable to face this horrifying tragedy in his life, Larry, the lifelong defense attorney who knew the workings of the criminal justice system like he knew where to buy his favorite cowboy boots, freaked out and ran out of the back of his house, scaled his backyard wall, whereupon he was seen by some very shocked and distressed neighbors. Finally, he was found in the parking lot of a local Albertsons store and brought home. The first thing she did was call Sarah Dutra and complain about him. Sarah took the next flight home from Italy to console her.

Still, the abuse didn't end. Laren told the police that she kept him doped up "because he wasn't capable of hurting me as long as he was strung out, and anyway, you know, I could get away from him."

But though she said she could get away from him, she also claimed she couldn't escape him. Searching such contrary points of view for any logic or evidence was difficult. As Elisa, Laren had managed the firm's money and traveled wherever and whenever she wanted. A lifetime of experience showed that if nothing else, she had become adept at fleeing if she found a situation not to her liking. To tell police that she was unable to escape the hell of being around Larry rang false.

At any rate, she said she was afraid of Larry, but not too afraid because she kept him doped up. She got him into rehab, and he busted out. He threatened to kill her, even taking a shot at her. Yet though supposedly he was violently out of control, she helped him escape.

Then it got even worse, she said, as Larry began doing eight-balls of cocaine and crack, taking Xanex and smoking heroin to come down off the coke, and drinking wine like a lunatic. "I walk in my house and every liquor bottle is empty and strung around the house. You know, that's craziness," she told the police.

It was hard for police to imagine that a man who was so meticulous his son and one of his daughters said he would never even leave an empty dish in a sink would be as sloppy and disorganized as Laren claimed.

"Dad never went to bed with dirty dishes in the sink. Ever, ever, ever," Tavia Williams said. "My dad was so immaculate there is no way that what the woman said ever happened. My dad could not handle having a single thing out of place. Not one dish in the sink."

Joe McNabney said he never saw anything like that at his father's house. "Dad used to cook for Elisa. He'd get home and take his time, and clean up right after. I know Elisa loved my dad and he loved her. When you saw them together, there was no way you could say they didn't love each other."

Not according to Laren's confession. By June 2001, she said, she was telling Larry she wanted to leave him, "and he would say that he was going to kill me or kill Haylei," she claimed. And so Sarah was coming home and helping her out, even when she was an exchange student in Italy, whenever Laren needed comfort and support.

The abuse got worse, and in a restaurant that summer he pulled a knife on Laren and threatened her again. Still, she said she could have taken it all, if it hadn't been for Larry's final act of desperation, which finally drove her over the edge to murder him. He'd already shot at her, threatened to stab her, choked her, beat her, screwed hookers in her presence, mentally abused her, and committed dozens of other venal and vile acts, yet Laren was hanging in like a trouper.

But that weekend in Industry City, she said, Larry went over the edge and threatened her dog, Munchie.

It turned out to be the fatal act. "He took my dog and hung him out on the balcony on the ninth floor, and he goes like, 'I'm gonna kill him' . . . you know, I was like, 'Don't kill my dog,' and there was a big fight and he brings the dog in and beats the crap out of me."

From there, she outlined how she and Sarah spoke on the phone, and Sarah rushed to her side to comfort her in her time of need, and that the two women cried and bonded and then decided to kill Larry because no one would miss him. Elisa talked to her friend about the cruel dog fiasco and showed Sarah bruises she claimed were inflicted on her. Then the two women began discussing options.

And Larry? According to Laren, he was already out in the horse trainer's shed stealing horse tranquilizer to feed his nefarious drug habit. He came back and crashed in his hotel room. Sarah hid from him, and then, as he was dozing away deeply, Sarah and Elisa approached the sleeping man and decided what to do. A few breaths later, as Laren spilled out her confession to an increasingly awestruck crowd of hardened police investigators, she said that she didn't actually say that she was going to kill Larry, but that she and Sarah just instinctively knew what to do because they'd spent so much time together. This made her angry because she didn't want to actually kill Larry; she just wanted to get away and thought she couldn't. She felt cornered, and that's when she and Sarah decided they had to kill him.

During the plotting, Laren claimed that one of them mentioned the horse tranquilizer only after they discussed the merits of smothering Larry with a pillow. Again, the investigators were stunned almost into silence as Laren in a precise and cold-blooded manner went about describing even a colder murder. She discussed alternative forms of committing murder as if she were trying to decide between paying with cash or a check. She sounded as void of emotion in killing her husband as exterminators are with killing ants.

But Laren did squirm a bit during the confession, shifting her weight back and forth, as if uncomfortable as she spilled forth the details of the murder. According to her, Sarah stood by the hotel room door while she leaned over the bed staring at Larry as they discussed killing him. Laren then bent over to see if his eyes were open or closed, and "he jumped out of bed. I mean jumped out of bed. Sarah's like screaming. And she runs out of the room. I run out of the room, and that's when we said, screw it and we went down to the trainer's truck . . ."

What happened next was a scene straight out of the movie constantly running through Laren's head. "We went down to my trainer's truck and I got the medicine bag out and I got the tranquilizer out of it, and I got a syringe, and I went back over to my truck and said, 'I don't know how we're gonna do it to him.' Sarah said, 'Put it in the Visine bottle,' so I squirted the stuff out of the Visine bottle and I stuck the syringe in there."

Suddenly, during her confession, the dam broke as Laren fully realized what she and Sarah did to Larry that day. In the middle of all the lies, the stories, the cover-ups, and the show came a moment of clarity. "Oh God, it seemed like a good idea at the time, but oh my God, it's so horrible," she cried.

Laren then described the entire macabre, drawn-out murder of Larry in vivacious and stark detail. She recounted the trip to Yosemite, Larry's struggle to survive, how Sarah hung him on a hook in his own truck, and then how they had to drag Larry into their house. She told about Sarah's trip to get her dog that night, and how Larry came to, bewildered, and struggled to leave the house, apparently knowing that he was dying and trying as hard as he could to get help.

"I guess I fell asleep," Laren said. "I heard the front door, and I thought, Oh my God. I run to the front door, look out, he's walking down the street."

Laren was stunned that Larry was still alive. She quickly ran out into the street and confronted him as he staggered away, struggling to stay alive. Panic may have played across his face as he stumbled forward, but he could barely walk and was no match for his wife at that point. He was nearly catatonic and probably scared beyond reason, knowing he had been poisoned.

Laren had Larry where she wanted him. "What are you doing?" she taunted. "Where are you going?"

"I'm gonna go die," he told her.

Laren easily ushered him back into the house. He was powerless to stop her. As she told the story to police, she claimed that she just wanted to take Larry back to the house to take care of him. Never mind that a man stumbling down the street screaming "I'm dying" might draw some attention to her murder plans. That never entered her mind. It was just a need to care for Larry that drove her to stop his flight. "I've always taken care of him when he was pissin' on himself and shittin' on himself. I was always cleaning him up, lying to the client, lying to the kids, saying he was at work when he's out sleeping with some black hooker."

Laren then took Larry upstairs and washed him up,

giving him the boxers and T-shirt he would be found in, and then as she was doing so, he had the audacity to "lunge" at Sarah when she entered the room. This angered both women. After all, Laren, according to her story, was trying to help out her lethargic husband, and he responded to her kindness by lunging at her best friend. So Laren told Larry he could sleep on the floor and she and Sarah left him.

"We don't want to kill him," Laren claimed. "We just want to be away. We don't want to kill him, we just wanted him to stop being so mean and so horrible."

She even contemplated calling poison control, but when asked by the police what stopped her from doing that, Laren said, "I wanted him to die."

She didn't call 911 because she was wanted in Florida and her best friend was involved in Larry's murder with her, and she wasn't sure Larry was all that bad off. "I've seen him in that kind of state 250 times. I've seen him in a worse state than that a hundred times now," so she wasn't even sure if she had killed Larry. Maybe she just got him high. When the police again questioned her point-blank about the inconsistency in her story, Laren didn't bat an eyelash. In her best, little girl, innocent voice she said, "I wanted to kill him."

"Right," said the officer.

"I wanted to kill him," Laren repeated.

"Well," said the police officer.

"Sarah wanted to kill him."

There, in a nutshell, was the essence of the prosecutor's case, laid bare with no pretense. It was as stark and as naked and as horrific as anything else done or said during the case. When questioned and called on the carpet about her lie, Laren broke it down to the simplest terms. She wanted Larry dead and so did Sarah. It is believable, next to every other lie Sarah and Laren told, for no other reason than the fact that Larry was dead by their hands. If actions speak louder than words, then the act of killing Larry spoke volumes.

"I'm totally prepared to, I know I'm gonna spend the rest of my life in prison," Laren acknowledged moments later. "Or to the electric chair or whatever it is you do with people. I mean, I know that. I know that I killed him and I know that I'm guilty and I'm prepared to deal with the repercussions of it."

She also said that she was then ready to deal with Larry's dead body. The next morning, when Sarah and Elisa found him dead and they were faced with what to do, they took almost no time to contrive a plan. They took the sheet Larry was lying on and wrapped it around him. Then "we took duct tape and wrapped it around him and he was like in a crouch position," she explained. They carried him down to the garage, where there was a refrigerator. Sarah cleared out the shelves and the two women hoisted Larry inside and unceremoniously dumped him there.

It was at this point that Tom Testa believes that if either woman had actually been thinking clearly, they could have possibly gotten away with the murder. Larry McNabney did have a drinking problem and was prone to bouts of depression. When they found Larry dead, had either woman called the police and said they thought Larry had suffered an overdose, they probably could have fooled everyone. Or, if Sarah had gone to the police the night before, when she took care of her dog, she could have successfully pinned everything on Elisa.

From there it was off to the races for Sarah and Elisa, as Laren described it. She outlined how they ran the business and tried to keep their heads above water. She spoke of the second attempt to get rid of Larry's body, which ended in a trip to Las Vegas and a dig in the hardscrabble desert ground north of the city.

In one of the most haunting parts of the confession, she discussed with police the pain and difficulty of digging a hole in the driving rain and putting her husband in that hole. She also talked about using scissors to cut off his clothes, and told everyone it was because Sarah told her there would be no DNA evidence if she did so. Although she claimed she was alone during this endeavor, she did at one point apparently slip and say, "We covered him up," but quickly added, "the best I could." When asked how deep the hole was, she offered a quip: "Obviously not deep enough."

Through it all, Laren took great time to detail exactly what she did and what she didn't do, as well as what Sarah did and didn't do. At times she sounded as if she lost control on the day Larry was murdered, saying time after time that Sarah calmed her down. "She was in control," Laren said. At other times she sounded firmly in control, claiming responsibility for killing Larry and the hell that went on in the office after he died.

It was a hell that ultimately engulfed everything around her, including her daughter, and as Laren sat in her jail cell, stripped of all pretenses, all illusion, and all wealth, she knew she had not done her best for Haylei. On March 18, 2002, she picked up a pen and wrote her daughter a letter. It is not only amazing in its content, but it is also incredibly lucid. There are eight pages of handwriting with hardly a strikeover or a mistake. The spelling is impeccable, as is the penmanship. Tom Testa considered it the most poignant piece of prose he'd ever read in regard to a murder case. For others it was sad, tragic, and ultimately painful to read.

Her father and mother said it was probably something Laren had been trying to write for years and could not, until she was done running and sitting in a cell.

Dear Haylei

I am so sorry for dragging you through the life I took you through. You have always loved me no matter what and that means everything to me. Since telling you the real truth about everything last night, I hope you can make your life good.

Don't steal and don't lie. I did both for as long as I can remember and look what I did to myself. Leaving you is the hardest thing I have ever done. I'm not doing it because I don't want to be with you. I am doing it so you can have your life. Today is the last day I will ever see you, so today is the beginning of your life.

My parents loved you so much when you were little, I can't imagine them turning their backs on you. They know I am the one who is bad, not you. I hope people don't judge you based on the things I did, but if they do, they don't deserve you. You have great friends and I know they will be a good support system for you.

I don't know if there is another life after this one, or

if there is a heaven. But, I do know if you live right, you won't have to face any more of the craziness you've lived with in your life.

I don't deserve to live and I can't live with the things I have done. I wish Sarah and I could go back and change the decisions we made, but it's too late. It is not too late for you. You have nothing to be ashamed of in this new life. You live it to the fullest. I am so proud of you. You are so smart and so beautiful and your heart is so good. Remember what I told you about school. If you go to the school and go to the financial aid office they will help you. I always took the easy way. Why earn it when I can steal it. You have to take the longer path. In the end it will be worth it.

When you get married, do it for the right reason: love. Don't do it because it's what you think you should do. There is a wonderful man out there for you. One who will love you completely. You will be able to have a family. I know how much you want children. You will be a fabulous mother. Your children will be so lucky. I hope you can have Cole in your life. I hope you can have a relationship with uncle Jason. He is a good man and he loved you so when you were young.

Keep writing, you have a special gift. You are talented and no matter the path, hold your head high and be proud of the person you are.

I wish I were strong enough to face all of this. I just don't feel like I deserve to live any more. If I am out of your life, you have a better chance of making it.

In the years that come, if you feel like you can't handle your life, get help. Keep asking, go to a hospital, go to social services, ask my parents, just get the help you need . . . I feel like I can't get everything out of me that I want you to know . . . You can open your heart now and not be afraid you will have to run. The running is over. No more fear every time a cop drives behind us or when the phone rings and there is no one there when you pick up. You don't have to be afraid of any of that stuff any more. When you feel afraid or doomed or crazy or suicidal, think of all we have gone through and you will make it. Try to let all of this into you without pain. This is your birth, your beginning. Not everyone gets a fresh start . . . I am too weak to face myself in the mirror every day. I hate myself for what I have done to you and everyone else around me . . . You must promise to tell the truth no matter what someone asks you. You are not aiding me, you are getting away from me after I told you everything last night.

I have to end my life because I have done such a bad job with it. By ending my life, I am washing you clean. You will have to live every day knowing your mom committed suicide, but you will know why and you will know that if there is a way for me to watch over you, I will be there. If you can try to hang on to my love for you, you will always have it. Along with my respect, admiration and loyalty, I will always be proud of you. You have made my life worth living. You are my sole reason for this path we are taking right now. This is the only thing I can give you. This is the start of your life. Don't be ashamed of your past. You can be ashamed of me. I deserve that. I hope one day you can forgive me.

Tell my mom and dad how sorry I am to have put

them through all of this. Please tell granddaddy I love him and please tell Cole I left him to protect him from me.

I love you, my princess. You are the most deserved person of all things good.

Go to your new life with my blessing and my deepest hope for health and happiness!

I will always be in your heart!

Love,
Mom

Of everything that Laren ever put in writing, or ever said to anyone, it was that letter that everyone felt was closest to the bone. It probably still contained some half-truths and lies, but it also included something that Cheryl Tangen said she noticed about Larry; in fact, both women said Larry was drawn to the darkness. Laren said Larry was unable to pull himself away from it, but it was her acts that drew him fatally close to her. And it was her darkness from which he couldn't extricate himself until Laren began feeding him the poison that slowly killed him.

"Larry always told me he thought he was going to die a violent death," Cheryl says. "He told me he wouldn't live to be very old and he would die violently. He told me once he was drawn to the dark side and couldn't help it."

Laren had finally come to the conclusion that she was at least partially to blame for Larry's death, and in so being the instrument of his demise, the darkness had gotten to her too. Staring into the abyss of what she had become, the spark of decency left in Laren—probably a residue of her feelings of love for her daughter—made her recoil from the woman she saw in the mirror.

But, even then, the threats of suicide in the letter didn't convince some of the police who worked the case. "I get a feeling," Deborah Scheffel says, "that Elisa was charming, charismatic, and high maintenance. She kept a foot in both the lower life-forms and in the silver spoons. She was sophisticated and manipulative. She had to have control, always. In the end, I think she committed suicide as one final act of control. She was a control freak to the very end."

Perhaps the detective was right about that, since, despite her assurances to her daughter that she was quickly going to end her life, Laren didn't do it right away. There were still other things to put in order, and she wasn't going to go anywhere until she had taken care of everything that she wanted. She still had several decisions and a few more actions to take.

Those final weeks were as shocking and surprising to her family and friends as anything else that had occurred in Laren's life. Some were even horrified by her actions.

For Laren Sims it was, in other words, life as usual right up to the end.

18

I Know This Was Right

When Tavia Williams heard Laren was in custody, she was ecstatic. "Right now the biggest emotion is happiness," she told a reporter. "We heard Friday that she was working in another law office, and you just have these fears. Now we know she can't do this to someone else."

Meanwhile, those in law enforcement, while not ecstatic, were at least pleased they'd finally found and captured the elusive con artist. Deborah Scheffel says that Laren was "one of the smartest criminals I've ever investigated. She not only survived but thrived for nearly a decade without proper ID, no credit cards, and nobody ever really caught on. It's simply unlike anything I've ever seen before."

Laren was held in Okaloosa County jail, which was quite a bit different from the home she'd been used to in California. Her existence changed from spending money lavishly and eating at the finest restaurants.

Now she got "three hots and a cot," as prisoners describe their daily regimen of three hot meals and a cot on which to sleep.

On March 20 she made her first appearance in court. Three Florida counties had a claim on her for her minor burglary, bad check, and parole violation charges, but California was hoping with her confession and cooperation that she would be extradited back to the West Coast. Her court-appointed public defender advised her not to sign anything, and so she didn't. That ensured that she would stay in Florida for a little while longer, but California officials were hoping to get her back to the Sacramento area within two weeks of her arrest.

As usual, Laren had other plans. She contacted Tom Hogan, her family's attorney, who had represented her so many years ago, and asked him for help. A tall man who, ironically, looks a little like the late Larry McNabney, Tom is also friendly and agreeable, and he wanted to help her out. He visited her in prison when he got the chance and tried to work on the case for her. "I caught her up with the family and what had gone on during the nine years she was away," he says. "I took her photos of the family so she could see how they had grown. As we were there talking, sometimes she forgot she was in jail and it was enjoyable."

But more often than not it was tedious. Laren was approaching the end of her rope and had already confessed plans of suicide to her daughter. Tom Hogan saw a strung-out woman. "She was exhausted, tired, and had been kept in isolation and wasn't allowed to shower. They were trying to break her down."

Hogan said the guards began working on her after she was transferred to the Hernando County facility in her hometown of Brooksville a few days after her arrest. The quaint old jail in a white stone house had by now been replaced by a modern facility run by the Capital Corrections Association. There would be no matronly visit from the sheriff's wife to feed Laren, and sometimes she felt like there would be no one around at all. It seemed to her that she was being singled out for retribution, and she told Tom as much.

She also told Tom her tale of woe about life with Larry, saying he was routinely drunk, angry, and had smacked her around. Tom said she gave up in jail and it was a sad thing to see her deteriorate before his eyes. But her life and the death of Larry McNabney weighed upon her heavily. "Ultimately murdering him was inconsistent with the rest of her life. Why didn't she just go?" he asked himself. He said she provided the answer, partially, by saying that she at one time confided her real history and prolems to Larry and he told her not to meet with Tom when he came out to Reno to straighten things out. After that, according to Tom Hogan, based on what Laren told him, Larry threatened to do harm to Haylei, so Laren didn't leave him. "Basically, she said Larry held Haylei hostage," Tom says.

"That just doesn't fit the facts," Tom Testa, who prosecuted Sarah Dutra, says. "On at least one occasion Haylei was in a boarding school three thousand miles from Larry McNabney. If she wanted to leave him, she could've done it easily enough then."

She opted, instead, to kill Larry.

By the time she made it back to her home county, Laren found out that her parents had picked up Haylei and were providing care for her. She was able to connect to her family and see how everyone had done in the decade since she'd disappeared. She wrote letters to her loved ones and put her affairs in order. Then, once she had settled everything to her satisfaction, Laren Sims had one more life to take.

Just around eleven-thirty a.m. on March 30, 2002, she committed suicide.

At the time, Laren was in an isolation cell, due to the nature of her crime, and while not specifically on suicide watch, she was supposed to be observed every fifteen minutes. According to the incident report from that day, nothing out of the ordinary had been seen in Laren's room that morning. But she had decided to play her last trick after forty-three-year-old deputy Vickie Price checked on her after eleven-fifteen.

At that time Vickie said she observed Laren reading a book and everything seemed okay. At eleven-eighteen Laren had a conversation with her guard asking if she could take a shower. Price told her that since Laren was going to be transferred—probably to California—very soon, she would have to wait. Vickie walked away to check on the paperwork for Laren's transfer. At 11:27 a.m. she opened the door to Cell HC7. It was a high risk room with a window that had blinds, a toilet, and a small bed. When Vickie opened the door, she found Laren hanging from a homemade rope of braided bed sheets. It was tightly woven and narrow. Frightened, she immediately called for help as she tried to remove Laren's weight from the rope so Laren could breathe.

Hidden away in the cell, they found Laren's last correspondence. Lurking inside a sandwich bag of discarded food, prison officials found a torn-up note in an envelope addressed to Tom Hogan. It consisted of seven pages of printed and handwritten material. It is a curious last letter, not as poignant as the one to her daughter written nearly two weeks before she died, but also filled with ultimately tragic and horrific news.

She began by telling Tom Hogan that Sarah Dutra's father had been in trouble with the law for embezzling money from the church where he had worked, and she revealed some personal information about Sarah.

Then she got into the abuse she suffered by Larry's hand, much as she had described it during her lengthy confession to police after her arrest. In the letter to Tom Hogan, she placed the date of the first beating exactly one year later than she did in her confession, saying July 2, 1996, was the day the horror show began. It coincided well with Tom's trip to meet Laren in Reno, so perhaps there was some reason to change the date. She also claimed to have a different witness in her letter to Tom. She doesn't mention Haylei being present at all, but said she called up a friend and the next day showed her the bruises, "on my back and legs. He always made the marks where they could be hidden."

She then gave Tom directions about how to get in touch with Larry's primary care physician to verify her claims, but then wrote, "Tom, I think we both know that it doesn't matter what kind of man Larry was, we murdered him. Of course I should spend the rest of my life in prison. Sarah should too. I wish I could change what happened, but I can't."

Then Laren turned her attention back to her daughter. "Bringing Haylei home was my chance to do something right. I did it. She has a family now. No matter what else I ever did, I know this was right."

Later she said that she was surprised her family even acknowledged her. To do so was "amazing. I am not good like they are. I do not have that in me. I don't know why and I don't know if I ever did. I just know I have always been a disappointment to them. I hope by bringing Haylei home, I tried to make them proud."

The guilt she felt about the life she led was evident on every page and with every phrase, but Laren also still couldn't resist turning the charm on one last time, telling Tom Hogan how she thought when she was a young girl how handsome he was and that "you were the man for me." Then she proceeded to give Tom advice about protecting and taking care of Haylei, as well as directions she would like to have Haylei follow once she was gone. She also advised Tom on how to do an interview with the television show *48 Hours* so her side "gets told," and then she came face-to-face with her own limitations: "I am not strong enough to face all of this. I have tried to dig deep inside myself and it isn't working. There is nothing left. I spent so many years trying to be strong and now I just feel empty."

She had a dying wish, though, and she wanted Tom to take up her cause. It was for Tom to sue the jail for allowing her to kill herself because she was in a high risk cell and was supposed to be checked every fifteen minutes, and she claimed she was not. Nor was she allowed telephone calls or showers, according to her claims.

She asked Tom to sue the private jail company, take the money and give it to her children. She ends her letter by thanking him for helping her and for looking after Haylei.

"Good luck with your life!! I feel enriched to have met you," she concluded, signing it, "Love Laren," and then with a small postscript, "Please tell my parents I love them."

With that last act, Laren signed out, penning her final submission in the screenplay that was her life.

She came to rest, briefly, on the floor of a cell made of three walls of cement blocks and the fourth of a metal framed glass with a door and a window with miniblinds. She didn't rest there long, since paramedics found a faint heartbeat and got her to the Brooksville Regional Hospital.

Detectives searched her body and found a bruise on her shin, a band tattoo around her ring finger, and a bright green frog tattoo on the top of her right foot. They found ligature marks and, along with the eyewitness account provided by the guard, came to the obvious conclusion that Laren had hanged herself.

She died shortly after five a.m. on Sunday, the day after she was found hanging from the rope, threaded through a ceiling air vent in the jail.

The case on Laren Sims, and her forty-seven or so aliases, was finally closed.

But the story of Larry's murder wasn't over yet.

19

Like Summer Camp

In February 2002 a detective working the case contacted an Internet pharmacy company whose name appeared on a credit card statement in the name of Greg Whalen. The records indicated that someone had ordered, with Whalen's credit card, a package of ten 100mg tablets of Viagra. While filing a fraudulent document report, Mary and Greg Whalen told police that they never even obtained the credit card used to make that and other purchases, nor did they authorize anyone to open the credit card account, especially not Elisa McNabney or Sarah Dutra.

Mary and Greg seemed convinced that Elisa and later Sarah were using them for purposes they didn't at first understand.

It became clear early on to police, however, what was going on. From the first time police questioned her on January 15, 2002, Sarah Dutra refuted Elisa's version of events that led up to Larry's murder, and she did her best to give police only as much as she had to. It was a push and pull effort with Sarah. You had to push her and then pull out the story, most of which it was later determined was invented in Sarah's own head in an attempt to save her own skin.

Initially, for instance, she wouldn't talk about going on the death ride through Yosemite with Larry, but she did volunteer that Elisa had two credit cards in her name, against her will. Logically, Sarah decided to give up Elisa, since obviously Elisa gave her up when she blew out of town with just her daughter Haylei. There were plenty of people claiming Elisa had forged their signatures, and later more would claim she had committed credit card fraud numerous times, so Sarah wasn't giving up anything the police didn't already have.

Sarah played cat and mouse very well, and was respected by those who prosecuted her. "I met my match in Sarah," said detective Deborah Scheffel. "Conducting the interview was difficult; she wasn't your average homicide suspect."

Her subtle cat and mouse game was seen in many different ways. For example, Elisa had said she showed Sarah bruises of the alleged abuse visited upon her by Larry. But Sarah told police she'd never seen Elisa and Larry have so much as a lover's spat.

She recounted how she met Larry and Elisa and how she'd been a faithful worker for them since 2000. She admitted that she had seen Larry at the Industry City horse show, but claimed not to know what had happened to him. She thought Larry and Elisa were getting along just fine. Sarah's story was different each time she was interviewed by the police, and she never gave up too much.

All of that changed once police decided to arrest her. They were suspicious of her story from the beginning, but Laren's confession, and ultimately the facts, led the police to conclude that at the very least Sarah Dutra was an able accomplice to the murder. She was picked up and charged with Larry's murder shortly after Laren sat down with detectives in Florida and spilled her swill for three hours and 132 pages of transcripts.

Once in jail, Sarah's demeanor changed dramatically. Her fellow inmates found her downright chatty and more than willing to talk about her high crime. She told one inmate that she poisoned Larry to prove herself to Elisa, and she laughed about the murder with another inmate.

After Laren took her own life, there was some immediate concern about how to proceed with Sarah's case. The San Joaquin County sheriff's spokesman in California, Nelida Stone, told the local papers that Laren's suicide wouldn't derail the investigation into Larry's death. "We still have a lot of unanswered questions and there is another person accused in this crime," she said.

At first authorities thought the motive of the crime was for financial gain, and they told many reporters that the pair took off with about $500,000 in cash. But Laren's trek across the country included the stops at homeless shelters as well as stops to gain employment. She obviously didn't have much money on her, and when she took her own life, she told Tom Hogan to sue the jail so her kids could have some money. Clearly, there was no nest egg, and whatever money the two women had stolen was long gone.

The question of why they ultimately killed Larry only confused investigators more. Why would Laren Sims kill Larry McNabney, the goose that laid the golden egg? All of her specious arguments of abuse and an inability to flee from Larry didn't add up. If Larry was drunk and didn't leave the house, as she claimed, she certainly had time to leave, especially when her daughter was away. And if he was as abusive as she claimed, then she still had time to get away on any of the road trips or during those days she had in the office when Larry wasn't around.

What began to make sense was a comment Tom Testa said that Greg Whalen made. Larry had told Greg that he caught Sarah "fucking his wife," and hearing that for the first time, investigators thought they had a more reliable picture as to what went on the last few months of Larry's life.

Beginning with her return from Italy, Sarah and Laren were inseparable, and it was making Larry increasingly angry. It made sense. Laren had separated Larry, systematically, from everyone in his life: both of his daughters, his son, his ex-wives, and friends, anyone she couldn't control and who posed a threat to her vampirelike need to suck Larry dry. Larry was lonely, with no one in his life but Laren, and when Sarah came back there was no one there at all for him.

Sarah was the catalyst in determining Larry's fate, and it was Sarah who provided the drive to complete the task.

"Who was Sarah Dutra? Take a look at Elisa Mc-

Nabney, that's who Sarah Dutra was," said Deborah Scheffel.

Bob Buchwalter, another investigator, said Sarah was just "a manipulative little bitch" and a "younger version of Laren Sims who never balked at doing anything for Laren."

Once arrested, police say Sarah initially showed little emotion. Later, when she did, it appeared to be manufactured to fit the moment. "Sarah? For someone so young, she was a very good liar," Scheffel says.

Buchwalter said that she and Laren were "kindred spirits," and that they also "fed off of each other."

Buchwalter, like Scheffel, was impressed with Sarah's ability to lie. "For example, she said she didn't go into the hotel room because she was afraid of [Larry]. But she described helping him into the truck and sitting next to him for a ride. That doesn't make sense. She lied right out of the gate. I'd ask her a question and she'd give me one answer. I'd reask the question a little later and she'd give me another answer. I knew she was involved from the beginning, but not how deep. She carried herself as a liar and she held her mud. She only gave up what we confronted her with. She never volunteered anything."

She also, apparently, didn't take her incarceration too seriously. A fellow inmate described her as looking forward to the bus trip to court as a field trip. She played games in jail with her cellmates, cutting out magazine pictures and hanging upside down from her bunk.

In the courtroom, she annoyed Larry McNabney's

family, who thought she had no respect for their dead father.

"I just got extremely angry," Tavia Williams says.

Cristin Becker Olson, Larry's oldest daughter, shunned the media glare that focused on the case, but expressed her displeasure with Sarah's behavior as well. "My father did not deserve this," she told the court. "Without Sarah Dutra's involvement, he would still be here today . . ."

Seeing Sarah fawn over her family and snicker and laugh at times put the McNabney family on edge. She had a similar effect on the police as they tried desperately to unravel what happened to Larry McNabney. He was dead. His wife was dead. And the only one left who was present at the time of the murder was a pathological liar whose self-interest in the case would predispose her to lying.

That's when Greg Whalen fell into place nicely as a patsy for her. There is some indication that Greg, affable and friendly, was being set up by Laren months before Larry died, just as there is evidence that Laren and Sarah planned and executed the murder over several months.

Riding with Greg to horse shows, talking to him on the cell phone incessantly, buying the Viagra all could have been part of an elaborate plot by Laren to set him up. There is the evidence that she pried loose the maiden names of Greg's and Mary's mothers. There is also the effort Elisa took with Greg. Perhaps even kissing him was part of her attempt to deceive and manipulate. Certainly, taking a man to bed wasn't beneath her. It would have been easy for Laren, who was used to manipulating younger, more successful, and better looking men into the sack. Luring Greg Whalen, a septuagenarian, would have been no problem for her, ethically, socially, or in any other way, as long as it helped her get what she wanted. She herself said, "Why earn it when you can steal it?"

With Laren out of the picture, it therefore became easier for Sarah Dutra to use Greg Whalen for her needs. She knew Laren well enough to know if she had been playing Greg, and how. Sarah was no slouch at deception, and using Greg as her patsy fit nicely with her plans.

Sarah became the innocent girl who was teased and taught how to behave by Laren Sims. Whalen became the co-conspirator who was bedding Laren and trying to keep Larry from knowing.

Naturally, it would lead to murder.

By the time Sarah was taken to jail and got defense attorney Kevin Clymo to represent her, she was firing on all cylinders.

Laren Sims had left Sarah Dutra stranded at the Sacramento airport, unwilling or unable to take Sarah on the road with her. Laren had played Sarah well, but Sarah was going to return the favor. She was going to use Laren for her own purposes, and it became easier with Laren dead. The bottom line for Sarah was that she was too young to turn herself off like Laren, and she had a much higher opinion of herself as well. She would not go gentle into that good night.

There was plenty of rage left in her against the dying

of the light and everything and everyone else. She had no intention of giving up yet.

She was young, and so even if she lost, she could appeal. She would be fine, or so she thought, if she could get someone to buy her story about Laren and Greg.

Greg's activities hadn't helped him.

He was obviously smitten with Laren in her alias of Elisa McNabney. He would later admit in court that he lied about taking furniture out of the McNabney home, and even had to admit he took the refrigerator that had been the coffin for his friend Larry for many months out of the house as well.

But members of the McNabney family also found him to be a kind and giving man, as did the prosecutors. None of them could believe that Greg Whalen would have anything to do with murdering his friend Larry McNabney.

Unfortunately, he was going to be dragged through the mud in a courtroom before anyone would come to understand that.

20

An Infested Wound

Sarah Dutra said she had recurring nightmares. In one of them, she was running away or running down a hallway from Elisa McNabney. Elisa "looked evil." Sarah always found herself looking for a safe place to hide, and right before she was captured, she would wake up to harsh reality.

According to her own admissions, her reality, before and after Larry died, was laced with excessive partying and heavy use of marijuana, diet pills, Ecstasy, and nitrous oxide. Perhaps it was hard to tell where the nightmare ended and reality began. Then again, knowing the extent to which Sarah and Elisa lied, it's hard to say that anything Sarah said about dreams, guilt, evil, or innocence was the truth.

Attorney Kevin Clymo tried his best to put a different face on Sarah. According to his defense, she was a wide-eyed innocent whose biggest mistake was walking into the McNabney law firm looking for a job in the summer of 2000. Once there, she fell under the influence of Elisa McNabney, and Clymo had no kind words for Elisa. "The McNabney woman," he said, "was a fugitive from justice. She had no true identity. She was one of the most manipulative women that probably anyone in this courtroom has even encountered."

Clymo's assertions did not sway Tavia Williams or Joe McNabney. During the many weeks of the trial they never once saw Sarah show any remorse for her part in killing their father. "She'd come in every day and wave to her dad and tell him that she loved him and it made me seethe," Tavia says. "She could do all of those things, and Joe and I couldn't do that. I idolized my dad. I would do anything to be able to tell him that I love him just one more time."

Sarah never seemed to care, one way or another. Nor did she show much concern or betray any emotions when Haylei took the stand to testify against her, even though almost everyone associated with the case thought Haylei held up well under questioning. "She was an extremely credible witness," Tom Testa said afterward. Deborah Scheffel, one of the lead investigators in the case, was as impressed with Haylei's ability to tell the truth as she was with her mother's ability to hide it.

Haylei, granted immunity in exchange for her testimony, told the jury that she had forged Larry's name on documents and had practiced forgery along with Sarah Dutra. She also testified that she knew from the time she was eight years old that her mother was on the lam and couldn't do things like buy a car, lease an apartment, or have a checking account. "I knew about my mom's previous record," Haylei told the court. But it didn't prevent her from loving her mother, even if they fought. The love between the two of them seemed uncompromising and unquestionable.

Haylei said she was just sixteen when her mother sent her to a Maine horseback riding school in September 2001 to "protect me" from Larry, who according to Elisa and Haylei was prone to fits of jealousy and bouts of drunkenness. She wasn't even on the scene when the murder took place, and that may have been coincidental to some, but it could have been engineered by Elisa, since she cared so deeply for her daughter that there was no way she would let Haylei either catch on to or see what happened at the Woodbridge home.

Laren's protection of Haylei remains one of the few indisputable facts about the case, and there is significance to it. Elisa lied to Haylei about her relationship with Sarah. They both lied to Haylei about their activities, and her mother lied to her about her own drug use and about the way she used men. But at the bottom of that, no matter what, Laren knew she was Haylei's mother. She lied and hid things from Haylei to protect her as well as to fool her. It was, perhaps, the only way Laren knew how to be a mother.

Haylei also told the court there had been problems between her and Larry McNabney. It wasn't difficult to see. Joe McNabney and Tavia—even in her limited exposure to Haylei—could see the reasons for that. "Dad didn't like liars," Tavia said time and again. And in Larry's and Joe's eyes, Haylei was also somewhat spoiled and every bit her mother's daughter, complete with a sarcastic attitude and the mouth of a typical teenage girl.

Haylei was almost relieved upon her return from the horse riding school when her mother told her that she and Larry had split up and that he had sought refuge in a religious cult.

The hell in which Haylei was raised was readily apparent as she testified in court. Her mother, constantly on the run and afraid of a past that would sneak up on her, unable to use her Social Security number and unable to get credit cards in her name, had only her wits by which to survive. It had been difficult at times, and Haylei betrayed little emotion as she said, "I don't claim to know why my mother did the things she did."

Haylei betrayed emotion only once. She dabbed at her eyes when she was asked to identify her mother in a picture showing Laren cheek-to-cheek with Sarah Dutra. It had to hurt her to know how close her mother was to Sarah. It also didn't jibe with Sarah's defensive stance that she lived in fear of Elisa McNabney. Haylei said she never saw Sarah afraid of her mother, and that Sarah was always willing to let her mother use her name to buy cars and make other purchases that typically needed identification.

This stood in direct conflict with Sarah's contention that Elisa was "evil" and manipulated and threatened her. When Sarah took the stand at the end of February 2003 to tell her side of the story, she laid it on thick. "Oh my God we've got to go to the police!" Sarah said she told Elisa after being summoned to the couple's bedroom where Larry was stretched out on the floor, apparently dead after a night of being poisoned by horse tranquilizer.

Sarah told a story similar to the one she told police between October 3 and November 20, 2002, when she described her fear of Elisa and of refrigerators and how she smoked a lot of marijuana because "it helped me forget. It made me numb."

The nightmares were haunting her still, especially a recurring nightmare in which she was running down a hall trying to get away from Elisa when she suddenly found herself in front of a refrigerator, opening it, only to see Larry staring out at her.

Compared to Haylei, Sarah was extremely emotional in the courtroom, rasping and sobbing as she described how she couldn't escape from Elisa, even as she drove away to take care of her small dog, and how Elisa forced her to help store Larry in the refrigerator.

From Sarah's perspective, she was as much a victim as Larry, perhaps even more so because Elisa had manipulated things so that she would take the fall for her.

But the real victim in the trial, other than Larry, may have been the septuagenarian horse trainer who Larry idolized, Greg Whalen. Kevin Clymo tried to paint Greg as a co-conspirator in Larry's murder. Naturally, the motive would be that Greg would want Elisa for himself, being lovestruck with the younger woman.

Greg did himself little good on the stand. He admitted to lying about hauling off the refrigerator, which had stored his dead friend Larry. He also claimed to be unable to recall certain details, trying to play himself off as a "befuddled" old man. But Kevin Clymo didn't fall for that act. He pointed out that when interviewed in the past, Greg had been able to remember details such as what Elisa had for dinner on a certain occasion. He also was able to get Whalen to admit that he told his workers to lie to authorities about going to McNabney's house more than two months after Larry disappeared and hauling off furniture, including the burial refrigerator in the garage.

Clymo was playing the shift the blame game, and Greg Whalen fell right into the trap. Part of the reason was his age, part of it because he was obviously infatuated with Elisa, and part of it was engineered by Sarah, who offered up some of the witness testimony against him. But then again, Haylei also painted Greg in a bad light, by testifying that he not only helped Elisa haul her horse trailer to Scottsdale, but tipped her off when authorities confiscated the trailer in Stockton, California. Haylei also testified that Greg helped her and her mother flee by giving Elisa $300.

Clymo made it quite clear where he was going. He had said in his opening statement that prosecutors had charged the wrong person, and suggested that Whalen supplied the poison to Elisa McNabney that eventually killed Larry. The motive again was love, lust, or a combination of the two. The purchase of the Viagra that made its way onto Greg's stolen credit card was further indication of his carnal desires, which manifested itself, according to Clymo, in helping Elisa with the murder. "It was Greg Whalen who helped Elisa get rid of the body and to hide the shovels," he said.

DUTRA'S DEFENSE POINTS FINGER AT TRAINER, the headlines in the paper screamed some three weeks into Sarah's trial.

Clymo's first witness as he put on his defense was Paula Mueller, an equestrian who was a regular at horse shows throughout the Southwest. She testified that she saw Greg Whalen and Elisa McNabney at a horse show in October, after Larry was killed, sharing a passionate embrace.

"Those people should get a motel room," Mueller said when she saw the pair. "They were kissing so heavily, the kissing caught my attention, and it went on."

Was Greg Whalen a victim of his seventy-year-old libido and a healthy dose of Viagra? Tom Testa tried to get Greg to admit on the stand that even if he was, it would be better to come forward with it than hide it. "I told him beforehand, whatever you do, don't lie to me," Testa said. Many figured Greg may have had a fling with Elisa, although he vehemently denied it and even threatened to sue those who insinuated as much.

For some it was a no-brainer to simply admit you'd had a fling with a woman half your age and be done with it. But Greg had an enormous amount of pride and was well thought of on the quarter horse circuit. Any whiff of scandal could destroy his reputation, and in a business where credibility counts and people have to believe you, it could be financially disastrous for him to admit to an affair. Because of those dual pressures, admitting any type of peccadillo with Elisa McNabney would have been beyond Greg Whalen's ability, even if it were true.

Whether or not he was involved with Elisa, for Tavia Williams it was inconceivable that Greg could have been involved with her father's death. "I know now some of what Greg and Dad talked about, and Dad was

very close-mouthed. For him to talk to Greg and to
confide in him the way he did, I can only conclude that
Dad cared a lot for Greg, and he obviously cared a lot
for my Dad."

Tom Testa had similar feelings. "I think Greg was
pretty much a straight shooter, who just got caught up
in things. He was a nice guy and he got used."

Naturally, Clymo painting Greg as a co-
conspirator didn't endear Greg Whalen to either him
or ultimately to the media. After the trial, he chased
away reporters on at least one occasion from his
ranch and routinely hung up on them when they
called.

As Kevin Clymo wrapped up his defense and proceeded with his closing statement, the picture he
painted for the jury was of necessity different from the
picture the prosecution painted, but ultimately so
bizarre that few could buy it. Elisa McNabney, growing bored with her husband, devised a plan to method-
ically poison him because he had become bothersome
and worthless to her. Then she drew in unsuspecting,
fun-loving college coed Sarah Dutra *to cover up* the
deed. According to Clymo, but for the evil that Elisa
embraced and foisted upon her, Sarah would have been
playing with her dog and painting surrealistic pillows.

Clymo said Dutra was scared and could have
avoided going to the authorities the day Larry was
murdered because she may have surmised it was use-
less to approach them about a murder when the whole
country was focused on the terrorist attacks at the
World Trade Center. According to Clymo, there was
simply no evidence to indicate that Sarah was any-

where near Larry McNabney when he was murdered, or that she ever had anything to do with poisoning him.

He made a very salient point in noting that the Mc-Nabney law firm had trouble years before Dutra ever came on board. There were the legal sanctions and check problems, and Dutra was never present when Elisa openly talked of spiking Larry's drinks with Vicodin and other drugs. Larry himself was arrested for drunk driving, and his practice, financial experts testified, was losing money long before Sarah came along.

"You can't beat Sarah up about that," Clymo said.

That picture was in stark contrast to the prosecution's view of Sarah. "All the evidence will show Elisa was capable of evil and Sarah participated with eyes wide open . . . in helping to kill Larry McNabney," said prosecutor Thomas Testa.

Testa's portrait of Sarah was not only one of a willing collaborator, but of a woman who drew closer to Elisa after the murder. They shared drinks, partied wildly, smoked dope, and shopped with wild, reckless abandon. They also shared clothes, slept in the same bed, and virtually lived together after Larry's death.

"That's kind of a special relationship," Testa said, tongue not so firmly planted in cheek.

If they weren't lovers, they were as close as two people could get, and all of their fun and games took place in a house containing a dead body in the refrigerator in the garage. How spooky, how macabre, and how horrible those conditions must have been, and yet for months the two women carried on while Larry very slowly decayed in the refrigerator. Far from being dominated, as Clymo contended, Testa painted a picture of Sarah as the stronger member of the relationship and the one who had the will and cold-blooded nature to pull off the murder.

Key to Testa's argument was what happened the night of the murder. As Larry was struggling through his last breaths on September 11, Sarah had taken Larry's truck—with Elisa's permission—to her parent's Vacaville home to retrieve her beloved dog, Ralphie. Certainly Sarah had the opportunity to call the police and possibly save Larry's life then, but she did not. No one was with her in the car then, and the only other occupant on the return ride was a small dog. Elisa wasn't there to stop her, and yet Sarah did nothing to harm Elisa that night, while at the same time she took actions to make sure Larry died.

"That's what you do when you're partners in crime," Testa said.

For four days in March 2003 the jury considered what to do with Sarah Dutra. It wasn't easy. She was young, she was good-looking, and she presented a sympathetic face to the jury. The jurors also didn't have a chance to see or read Laren's long confession because the judge had ruled that it was inadmissible as evidence. Inside the jury deliberation room the facts they did have to ponder were tantalizing and yet confusing. Many jurors thought Sarah was involved with murdering Larry but were unsure to what extent. Eleven of the jurors had agreed upon a second-degree murder conviction, which would have meant fifteen years to life in prison. But according to the *Sacramento Bee*, there was one holdout who insisted Testa had not proved that Dutra intended to murder Larry.

"None of us wanted to see Sarah go unpunished and walk away from this," said forewoman Patricia Thayer, a third grade teacher. "At one point, we thought we were going to be hung . . ."

No one on the jury wanted that either, because they didn't think the prosecution would retry the case if they couldn't reach a decision, and everyone, even the holdout, wanted Sarah to serve time for her involvement in Larry's death.

On March 19, 2003, the day before the United States started a war with Iraq, the jury settled on manslaughter, which meant Sarah faced a maximum of 11¾ years in prison. Even if she served every day of her sentence with no time off for good behavior, she would still be younger than Elisa McNabney when she got out of jail. With the possibility of parole and good time, she could leave prison and be about the same age Elisa was when she first met Larry.

Superior Court Judge Bernard Garber then had the responsibility of sentencing Sarah. Nearly a month passed before she would find out how long she would have to serve in prison, if indeed she would have to serve a day there. Kevin Clymo had requested probation for his young client.

There was much to consider for Judge Garber. Sarah's age, her lack of a criminal history, and more than two dozen letters of support all weighed heavily in her favor. Other than her father's church embezzlement troubles, there was little to indicate that Sarah would be a problem, and her family had stood by her.

For Tavia Williams that was the biggest slap in the face. She asked to write and read into the record a let-

ter to Sarah, and the judge allowed it. In part this letter
said:

> *There are no words that can express my deep feelings
> of loss, sorrow, and sadness over our dad's murder.
> Nothing can ever replace the wisdom, advice, and love
> our father gave and how he touched our lives. These
> precious gifts are all we have to sustain us for the rest
> of our lives.*
>
> *There have been few nights in the last sixteen
> months when I haven't quietly cried myself to sleep or
> awakened in the middle of the night crying. Sarah, I
> want you to know that in every tear, there is a river of
> sorrow and memories. In every tear there are oceans
> of love and loss.*
>
> *Every day we sat in court, you would smile and wave
> at your dad, showing no respect or remorse to Joe and I
> for this unthinkable act. Even while they showed pic-
> tures of our dad with body parts sticking out of the
> ground or the tapes that would describe what the two of
> you did to our dad, there was never evidence by your
> body language that you were sorry or even cared . . .
> you again showed no remorse. You sat and watched and
> were involved in the taking of a human life—our dad's!!*
>
> *How could a person with a soul or conscience drive
> with our dad alive, knowing that he was slowly being
> poisoned? You had the choice and opportunity to do
> something—and you chose murder over life! It pains
> me to think you were one of the last people to see my
> dad alive. You took that away from me.*
>
> *Our family time on holidays, graduations, and such
> will never again include our dad; it will only be us*

*gathering by his graveside. Sarah, you have robbed us
of years with our dad. We can never get a simple hug,
a kiss, a glance, or even hear his voice again. Sarah,
you have stolen these simple pleasures of life from us.
I pray that every time you see your father or think of
him, that you will remember what you took from us.*

*We will make it through this, and I pray that this
horrific injustice never has us stop believing that our
faith, inner strength, and the power of God's love will
carry us through.*

On Monday, April 21, 2003, at eight-forty a.m.,
Judge Garber's court convened to consider Sarah's
sentencing. Before him was a motion by Kevin Clymo
for a new trial based on the way the court gave its instructions to the jury. It was a purely technical motion
that Testa objected to because it was filed at the end of
the business day on April 18, and the judge ultimately
denied the motion.

The next thing to consider was Laren Sims's confession. Tom Testa wanted it as a part of the record for
sentencing, while Clymo did not. It had already been
kept from the jury during the trial, and while Testa had
objected to it, he understood why it was kept out of evidence. But the rules were different for sentencing, and
Testa thought it was relevant in considering what sentence to impose upon Sarah Dutra.

"We have already had a hearing on this when Elisa
McNabney made her statement in Florida, she expressed concern for Sarah's welfare. 'How is Sarah doing? I'm glad she's okay.' The Court remembers that,"
Testa said.

"And she also went out of her way to say, 'No, Sarah did not help me bury the body.' If she were going to burn Sarah, that would be the time to do it. She would say, 'Oh yes, Sarah was there with me.' "

According to Testa, the information was relevant because it pointed out that Sarah did indeed help Elisa execute the murder, and that it was Sarah who hung Larry on a hook in the truck while his arms flailed about in a futile attempt to fight back against the women who were murdering him.

The judge, however, had a big problem with Elisa's confession. It was the one time when, in her father's vernacular, she was going to have to pay the tab for what she'd done. The judge simply didn't know what to believe in her confession. Often, deathbed confessions are the exception to states' hearsay laws. But as the judge watched Laren's tape, read the transcripts, and listened to the testimony, he could do nothing more than shake his head at what he read, saw, and heard.

". . . There are certain facts in that they are corroborated," the judge said from the bench, "and I'm sure there are certain things that she was being truthful about. But the other statements where she directly implicates the defendant in the actual killing of the victim, I have wondered and wondered was that true. And my answer is: I don't know.

"I mean, her life, you talk about a life being a lie, that was Elisa McNabney. And while I still stand by my ruling in allowing it at the prelim, I would never have allowed this to get in front of a jury. And it was . . . just obviously inadmissible as far as a jury seeing it because . . . of the significant hearsay issues.

There's no right of confrontation and cross-examination, which is a very fundamental Constitutional right that every defendant has . . . they say that a dying declaration is admissible because most people aren't willing to meet their maker with a lie upon their lips. I don't think that would apply to Elisa McNabney.

". . . I don't think anything would prevent her from making a final lie. And so, I don't know what her motivations were in making this statement."

Clymo seized upon the judge's ambivalence to argue for probation. "I believe that this is an exceptionally unusual case," Clymo said. "Miss Dutra, for a lifetime prior to her contact with Elisa McNabney and Larry McNabney, led a law-abiding life. She was an honor student in high school. She was an honor student throughout the college program that was interrupted by this arrest, and she's never had so much as an arrest prior to her involvement in this case."

According to Clymo his client was just one big festering boil until detective Deborah Scheffel squeezed out the poison. "She popped like a wound, like an infested wound, and the infestation began to drain," Clymo said with a straight face.

Clymo was much more to the point about Elisa McNabney and her effect on Larry, giving perhaps in the shortest number of words the most accurate description of her character: "Elisa McNabney began killing Larry McNabney in the state of Nevada when she took his respectability, when she took his money, when she robbed him of contact with his daughter. Sarah had nothing to do with that. That was years before Sarah ever walked in that law office and asked for a job."

Inadvertently making a strong argument for naming Sarah as a catalyst for what happened to Larry, Clymo nonetheless hit on an important point often missed by Larry and desperately missed by those closest to him. Elisa McNabney began robbing Larry blind from the moment she entered his life. She stole his steady girlfriend, who adored him and said he never struck out in a mean fashion against her. She stole Tavia Williams and daughter Cristin from Larry. She robbed his son of any effective means to assist his father. She stole money. She stole prestige; a lifetime reputation built on trust and good faith as well as hard work. She stole his credit, she robbed him of his dignity, his humanity, and ultimately even of his life. She sucked Larry completely dry. For those who doubt that vampires exist, prosecutor Tom Testa said he had found one: Laren Sims starring as Elisa McNabney in the macabre nightmare that she spun in her own head.

"Is there any crueler way to die than to know you are dying, but you are too lethargic to do anything about it? To be kind of semiconscious? Somebody is putting drops in your mouth as you are being driven through Yosemite. You know you are dying. You are saying, 'You are not going to get away with this. You are not going to get away with this.' You say this about ten times, but you are too weak because of the poison to stop the two people that are killing you. I can't think of a worse way to die."

But further, Testa saw Sarah Dutra as a vampire as well. "If anything, Sarah Dutra kind of wore the pants in the house, so to speak," he explained. "People that saw them on a daily basis, for example Ginger Miller, said . . . Elisa would freak out, Sarah Dutra was the logical one. [She] would say, 'We'll figure it out. We'll work this out. You want me to get a man to call, pretend he's Larry?' Sarah Dutra was the one that was . . . most of the time in charge of things . . . there was never any fear around Elisa. 'She's never threatened me.' These are quotes from her statements. 'I'm all about having fun. We had a good time together.' Not one iota of fear did this court hear from her mouth or from any of the witnesses."

Testa also took time to point out that Sarah and Elisa had discussions well before September 11 about killing Larry, so any claims that Sarah had about being a passive participant was also another exercise in Orwellian logic. Elisa told Sarah that she didn't want Larry around, and the two women discussed different ways of getting rid of him. "She said she wanted to kill him and I said, 'Okay. Do it,' " Testa said, quoting Sarah.

Testa also pointed out the scorn and derision Sarah had for Larry, telling police plenty of blatant lies that she knew to be untrue whenever she got the chance. " 'Oh, he was out getting hookers. He was using drugs. And he used to beat her.' Things that she knew were not true, she was just lying about."

She had lied to Elisa's daughter. She lied to friends, family members, clients, complete strangers—anyone and everyone.

Finally, in deciding what to do with Sarah Dutra, the judge listened to Larry's daughters and his son who were allowed to make statements. They all spoke of not being able to see their father anymore and how Sarah had been a part of it and had lied to them on numerous

MARKED FOR DEATH   285

occasions. Only after listening to all of that and looking over Laren Sims's confession did the judge begin ruminating on what he would do.

"The most significant factor for the defense is that she has no prior record, and this is always an important factor," the judge said. He discounted Sarah's later admission of wrongdoing coupled with limited remorse because of previous statements in which she lied. "There were a number of inconsistencies, a number of lies. And it was a significant time before she finally did make the admissions she did make."

Based on that, and a negative probation report that pointed out some of Sarah's more outlandish activities while being incarcerated, the judge denied Sarah's appeal for probation.

As he considered what sentence to deliver, the judge said further, "There was this incredible pattern of lying, cheating, stealing, and forgery. We have the testimony she was practicing forging the victim's signature over and over and over again in this notebook, which was received in evidence. I can't recall ever having heard that type of testimony before . . . To me, it just shows a sociopathic personality."

The defining moment of the trial for the judge came when the tape was played describing the scene of taking Larry's body down the stairs and into the refrigerator in the garage. In it, Laren described the morning where she and Sarah took the body from upstairs in the Woodbridge home into the refrigerator. With very few differences, it was essentially the same testimony offered by Sarah. The two women had, in cold blood, simply wrapped Larry up in a blanket and deposited him in a refrigerator. That uncontested fact turned the judge's stomach.

"It's just chilling listening to that," the judge explained. "You could hear a pin drop in this courtroom."

He was undeniably shaken by listening to the further testimony. "So, the body is there for three months. And during that time, the defendant is staying off and on at that house. I just can't imagine what it would be like under those conditions, knowing that there's a dead man in the refrigerator in the garage. And she's there off and on. They're going to horse shows, doing this, doing that, shopping, buying things . . . and then, in the middle of it, the two of them go to Las Vegas in a red Jaguar convertible with a dead body in the trunk. I just don't—I can't imagine that. Then they come *back* from Las Vegas with a dead body in the trunk."

Sarah Dutra was done. Had the judge been able to sentence her to more, he would have. But as it was, he gave her the maximum sentence and left it at that.

There was a resounding and spontaneous explosion of cacophonous applause as the judge read his sentence. Tom Testa, for one, was not that happy. "She is a murderer and she should have been convicted of murder. I respect the jury's verdict, but it doesn't change what happened." At the trial he urged the judge to "throw the book" at Sarah.

Upon hearing the sentence, Garey Zimmer, one of the jurors, told the local press, "I wish we would have done our job. The judge did his. But we just didn't have all the information that would have made it possible for the murder conviction."

The March 30 edition of the *Sunday Record* was

even blunter. DUTRA JUROR: 'I WAS DUPED' screamed the headline. This was even before the sentencing. In that article, Garey Zimmer said he was duped, and other jurors said they wished they could have heard at least the testimony of one jail inmate who Testa said would have testified that Dutra bragged in jail that she actually administered the fatal dose to McNabney to prove herself to Sims.

The jurors joined a long line of people who felt they were conned by Laren Sims and Sarah Dutra. They told the judge and reporters that it would be a long time before they felt okay with themselves after hearing some of the more damaging testimony not allowed in court.

In the end, Larry McNabney was dead. Laren Sims was dead. Ginger Miller had split, hopefully never to see or hear of the events that drew her into court ever again. Sarah Dutra was in jail. Only Haylei got away with a fresh start.

Living in a log home out in the country, miles from a big city, was the environment in which Laren Sims grew up. She never appreciated its values until the very end of her life, when she struggled so desperately to get her daughter back to her parents.

Now legally an adult, Haylei has a chance to change her life and go down the path her mother wished she had followed but never did. She's getting that chance because of the sacrifice her mother made. It will be interesting to see what she does with it.

As for Sarah Dutra, perhaps one of the investigators put it best when he said, "What will she do when she gets out of jail? How will she get a job and what can she put on her resume: 'Helped to murder previous employer'? I pity the man who runs across her path when she gets out."

The last chapter has been written on Laren Sims. Her time has expired. But the fear of some is that Sarah Dutra may just be getting started.

"Vampires do exist," Tom Testa says. "Don't be fooled."

Sarah Dutra appealed her conviction. Oral arguments were heard in March 2005.

THE LAST GANGSTER

From Cop to Wiseguy to FBI Informant:
Big Ron Previte and the Fall of the American Mob

0-06-054423-6/$7.99 US/$10.99 Can

For thirty-five years, "Big Ron" Previte roamed the
underworld, a capo in a powerful Philadelphia-South Jersey
crime family. But by the 1990s, as Previte saw it,
the days of loyalty and honor were over, and he became
the FBI's secret weapon in its war with the Philly mob.

THE GOODFELLA TAPES

The True Story of How the FBI Recorded a
Mob War and Brought Down a Mafia Don

0-380-79637-6/$6.99 US/$9.99 Can

In Philadelphia in 1993 an embittered legacy of rivalry
and hatred exploded in a brutal, bloody battle between
old world mobster John Stanfa and the young, flamboyant
Joey Merlino. However, this would be warfare different
from any other because this time, the FBI had it
down on tape.

GEORGE ANASTASIA has been a reporter
Philadelphia Inquirer for more than a
has been nominated twice for the